T0079745

SAUSAGE

Edible

Series Editor: Andrew F. Smith

EDIBLE is a revolutionary series of books dedicated to food and drink that explores the rich history of cuisine. Each book reveals the global history and culture of one type of food or beverage.

Already published

Apple Erika Janik *Barbecue* Jonathan Deutsch and Megan J. Elias *Beef* Lorna Piatti-Farnell *Beer* Gavin D. Smith
Brandy Becky Sue Epstein *Bread* William Rubel
Cake Nicola Humble *Caviar* Nichola Fletcher
Champagne Becky Sue Epstein *Cheese* Andrew Dalby
Chocolate Sarah Moss and Alexander Badenoch
Cocktails Joseph M. Carlin *Curry* Colleen Taylor Sen
Dates Nawal Nasrallah *Doughnut* Heather Hunwick
Dumplings Barbara Gallani *Eggs* Diane Toops
Figs David C. Sutton *Game* Paula Young Lee
Gin Lesley Jacobs Solmonson *Hamburger* Andrew F. Smith
Herbs Gary Allen *Hot Dog* Bruce Kraig *Ice Cream* Laura B.
Weiss *Lamb* Brian Yarvin *Lemon* Toby Sonneman
Lobster Elisabeth Townsend *Milk* Hannah Velten
Mushroom Cynthia D. Bertelsen *Nuts* Ken Albala
Offal Nina Edwards *Olive* Fabrizia Lanza *Oranges* Clarissa
Hyman *Pancake* Ken Albala *Pie* Janet Clarkson
Pineapple Kaori O' Connor *Pizza* Carol Helstosky
Pork Katharine M. Rogers *Potato* Andrew F. Smith
Pudding Jeri Quinzio *Rice* Renee Marton *Rum* Richard Foss
Salmon Nicolaas Mink *Sandwich* Bee Wilson *Sauces* Maryann
Tebben *Sausage* Gary Allen *Soup* Janet Clarkson
Spices Fred Czarra *Sugar* Andrew F. Smith *Tea* Helen Saberi
Tequila Ian Williams *Truffle* Zachary Nowak *Vodka* Patricia
Herlihy *Water* Ian Miller *Whiskey* Kevin R. Kosar
Wine Marc Millon

Sausage

A Global History

Gary Allen

REAKTION BOOKS

This little book is dedicated to my late mother, Arline 'Billie' Allen (and to her mother, whom I never met, since she died five years before I was born). Together, they instilled in me a taste for their 'League of Nations' approach to cooking and eating, and a lifelong curiosity about so-called foreign foods.

Published by Reaktion Books Ltd
33 Great Sutton Street
London EC1V 0DX, UK

www.reaktionbooks.co.uk

First published 2015

Printed and bound in China

A catalogue record for this book is available from the British Library

ISBN 978 1 78023 500 4

Contents

Introduction

Four decades ago, before there were any books available on sausage for the home cook, I became interested in sausage-making. Having discovered that there was little written on the subject, I began researching the topic myself, converting commercial-scale recipes to manageable size, and participating in every part of the process, from slaughter (yes, even cleaning out pig intestines for casings – which, as you can imagine, was not one of the more pleasant parts of the research) to finished dishes. That was before I was a writer, and no book ever came out of it. Since that earlier start, many sausage cookbooks have been published, so *this* book takes a different approach: historical and comparative. It attempts to help us understand a little about where our sausages come from, and how they got to be the way they are today. While I was undertaking my early research, every dinner guest at my home was subjected to one sausage dish or another. In the course of writing this book, the process has been repeated, perhaps – as dinner guests might have been too polite to say – ad nauseam. It is probably impolitic to refer to those long-suffering diners as guinea pigs, but I am nonetheless grateful for their sacrifice.

Sausages have long been part of our gastronomic lives, probably for as long as humans have used fire and salt to

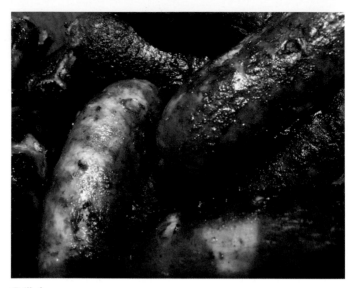

Grilled sausages.

prepare food. They have been invented, independently, in many places. Specific sausages have also been introduced to other cultures, gradually evolving in the presence of different conditions, cultures and ingredients.

What makes a sausage a sausage? What doesn't? These are fundamental questions, and the answers are, at once, as simple and as varied and complex as anything in the gamut of world foods. It is the opposite of the famous remark, often misattributed to Otto von Bismarck, that 'the making of laws is like the making of sausages – the less you know about the process, the more you respect the result.'

This book celebrates sausages in all their spicy, salty, smoky and juicy glory. While it may not earn respect for these once-humble foods, it may elicit greater appreciation for their vast savouriness and variability, and reveal the way they (and we) have spread around the globe.

I

What is Sausage, and Where Did it Originate?

When our early ancestors began to coordinate their hunting activities, giving them access to large animals – at least ones that were not already dead when they found them – they had to deal with a number of new technical problems. First was the size of the prey. The need to cut the fallen beasts into more convenient parcels led to the creation of better cutting tools, and bone, horn, stone and even fire-hardened wood provided the raw materials for a host of cutting and scraping implements. Second came spoilage: meat is one of the most perishable of foods, and early humans learned that smoking and drying could extend the period of time in which meat remained edible and safe. Our oldest written records show that we have long known that salt improves the quality and longevity of preserved meats. Surviving Sumerian clay tablets from Mesopotamia (1600 BC) are filled with references to salted meats.[1] The third problem was packaging and the avoidance of waste. Hunting large animals involved considerable effort, and so it was critical that none of the animals' flesh or organs be wasted. Somewhere in our ancient past, a hunter realized that the intestines, stomachs and skins of animals could be fashioned into convenient parcels for all the scraps of meat and organs that might otherwise be wasted.

It was inevitable that those three sets of considerations would lead to the creation of what we now know as sausage. The savoury links have been invented, independently, in many parts of the world, and recipes and techniques have accompanied humans everywhere we have travelled. According to the food historian Maguelonne Toussaint-Samat, 'It may fairly be said that the sausage-making tradition has survived uninterrupted for 200 years in both Rome and France, and the sausages themselves have remained much the same.'[2]

While the facts of the creation of the first sausage are lost in ancient times, we do know that it occurred at least 3,000 years ago. We know from murals that the ancient Egyptians made a kind of sausage from the blood of sacrificial cattle, but two of the earliest *written* accounts of sausages appeared in Homer's *Odyssey* (eighth century BC):

> Here are goat stomachs ready on the fire
> to stuff with blood and fat, good supper pudding,
> The man who wins this gallant bout
> may step up here and take the one he likes. (Book 18, lines 16–19)

and

> Rolling from side to side
> as a cook turns a sausage, big with blood
> and fat, at a scorching blaze, without a pause,
> to grill it quick. (Book 20, lines 24–7)

It is significant that each of these early accounts refers to blood sausage, a style that reflects the 'no-waste' attitudes of the past but is today found only in certain ethnic cuisines (and, increasingly, among adventurous 'gourmet' consumers). The accounts also reflect the long use of goat – one of the most-consumed meats on the planet – and beef in sausages, a fact that is easily overlooked when we think of pork as the ideal forcemeat.

The practicality of sausages, no doubt, led to their independent invention in many places and, indeed, they are found almost everywhere. Some, as we shall see, have migrated with us to new places and evolved into new variants as a result. Ingredients and methods have often changed in response to local conditions and taste. The number of possible variations on a seemingly simple culinary theme may not be infinite, but it is very large indeed.

Exactly what sausage *is* can be difficult to state precisely. The broad category of charcuterie includes many sausage-like foods, and many that are not sausage at all. When we try to parse the exact details that make, or do not make, something 'sausage', we are stymied by contradictions and exceptions. As the American Supreme Court Justice Potter Stewart famously said of obscenity, he cannot define it, but he knows it when he sees it.

Aix-en-Provence's market in the Place des Prêcheurs.

Sausages may be simple patties of chopped, seasoned meat. In fact, one of the oldest specific sausage references was to the Roman *insicia*, a name derived from the Latin word for chopped meat (which was, in turn, derived from the Greek *isikion*, which referred only to chopped meat; the Greeks' generic word for sausage was *alla*). Our recipes, and the words we use to describe them, have very long genealogies. While cookbooks (when they exist) can tell us when dishes were first committed to writing, sometimes the names of the foods themselves can tell us about how and when they came to be.

Spanish *lomo* and Italian *prosciutto* are obviously forms of charcuterie – being cured chunks of pig flesh – but they are not sausages. The protein of sausages is always cut up in some way, then bound back together. A ham cannot be considered sausage. In some sausages, such as liverwurst or bologna, the particles of flesh are so small as to be indistinguishable. In others, the pieces are large and cleanly cut, like the cubes of pork in brawn (known in the u.s. as headcheese), or really huge, like the hunks of ham in *culatello* – but they are always bound together in a shape they did not have before.

Sausages are eaten fresh, or after being dried, fermented, smoked or any combination of these techniques. Some are meant to be cooked, using any of the traditional methods for cooking meat (baking, boiling, frying, grilling, roasting), while some are so heavily cured, dried and/or smoked that they can safely be eaten raw (*salame crudo*), because their water content is too low for harmful bacteria to survive.

Encased or Not?

Forcemeats are commonly stuffed into casings (although some are formed into patties or used loose). Is a skinless frank less of a sausage than a traditional hot dog that snaps when you bite into it? Is a casing even an essential part of the definition of a sausage? Could meatballs not be considered a form of un-encased sausage? After all, they are formed of well-seasoned forcemeat, just like sausage. What about quenelles? For that matter, what about the vast variety of forcemeats that come encased in dough, such as Chinese dumplings, Italian ravioli, Latin American empanadas, and so on? Perhaps the only reason for *not* including them all in the sausage tribe is the matter of space available in a book like this.

Mortandela affumicata della Valle di Non, from the Italian region of Trentino-Alto Adige, sounds like *mortadella*, but is actually a meatball of pork flesh and offal, rolled in buckwheat flour and smoked. *Boulettes*, French meatballs, can be made

The wall of fame at Hot Doug's Sausage Superstore, Chicago, Illinois.

Pitina, or *pettuce*, a classic Friulian sausage, originally used chamois, goat or sheep (this one is lean beef and pork belly) – it's formed into a patty, rolled in cornmeal, lightly smoked and aged for three weeks.

from any forcemeat, and are found in many Francophone regions. In Morocco, they are made of *merguez*, while in Louisiana, chicken, crab or prawn (or any combination thereof) is used. Dutch and Belgian *frikandellen* are sausage-shaped forcemeats, eaten like sausages. Romanian *mitiei* (garlicky beef, with caraway, cayenne, paprika and thyme, cooked on skewers) reflect their historical link (via the Ottoman Empire) to today's Middle Eastern street food.

What about sausage-like foods that are neither encased nor formed into balls or patties? German *Leberkäse*, brawn, scrapple and American olive loaf are cooked (and/or cooled) in loaf tins before being sliced. Some German *Kochwurst* is poured into jars or cans, which are sealed, then boiled or cooked in steam. *Schickensülze* is a high-quality brawn made from cubes of cooked ham with concentrated gelatine, poured into loaf tins, then left to cool and solidify (*Schwartenmagen*, another brawn, is available in cans). Does that mean Spam – seasoned, cured, finely minced pork, cooked in its iconic blue can – is a sausage?

If we do not exclude some of these forms of charcuterie, the definition of sausage becomes too broad to be of any use. We can narrow it through a process of elimination, however. Meatballs should be excluded, unless they are wrapped. Also any cold meat that is formed into loaves (such as those listed above, as well as meatloaves, galantines, terrines and pâtés, which are more appropriately products of *garde manger* than charcuterie), with the possible exception of brawn. Finally, we must exclude Spam, because the less we have to think about that pink stuff, the better (and even the company that makes it considers it to be a form of ham).

The most common meat used in sausages is pork, because its flavourful fat provides succulence and cures well, although almost any sort of protein will do as long as it contains enough fat to maintain a juicy product. Beef, chicken, duck, many kinds of game, goose, horse, lamb and mutton, mule, seafood (both fin fish and shellfish) and veal have all been made into sausages. Game, such as venison or rabbit, tends to be very lean (or the fat is unsuitable, owing to its flavour or melting properties), so pork fat or beef suet is usually added. Chicken, duck and goose have more than enough fat, but it melts away too easily to provide moist sausage, so pork fat is generally added to them as well when permitted by religious rules; obviously, kosher sausages do not contain any pork products. Vegetarian sausages have even been made from gluten and soy proteins. A typical sausage recipe consists of protein plus 20–30 per cent – sometimes as much as 50 per cent – fat by weight. In some sausages, such as *mortadella*, visible chunks of fat are added after the meat and seasoning have been emulsified, as a garnish.

Sausages generally contain salt; indeed the word 'sausage' is derived from Latin *salsus*, 'salted'. Salt serves three functions in sausage: it helps to preserve the meat, binds the bits of protein together and adds flavour.

Other than salt, sausage seasonings vary according to ethnic cuisine. Black pepper is common; basic fresh Italian sausage contains only pork, salt and pepper (although Italian sausages made in the USA generally include fennel seeds and red pepper as well). Garlic perfumes sausages in many cuisines, including those of Germany, Hungary, France, Latin America, Poland, Portugal, Spain and the USA. Chilli pepper, in many forms (dried flakes, cayenne, paprika – hot or sweet – or smoked, as in Spanish *pimentón*), appears in sausages around the world. Sausages from northern cuisines typically avoid hot chilli, although they tend to be served with mustard, since their richness cries out for a pungent condiment to cut through all that fat. Breakfast sausages, eaten fresh in the USA, usually contain sage, and often marjoram. Cloves, cinnamon and nutmeg tend to be used in black (blood) sausages. Chinese sausages, *lop cheung*, are sweet, containing sugar, soy sauce and five-spice powder (a mixture usually consisting of ground cassia, cloves, fennel seeds, star anise and Sichuan pepper – named not for its variable list of ingredients but for the fact that it contains all the Chinese flavour components).

While not all sausages are encased meats, most are forced into some sort of casing. Natural casings are most common, usually obtained from the internal organs of one animal or another – not necessarily of the species that provided the main ingredient.

Sausages are often dried by being hung in cool, circulating air, preserving them and enhancing their flavour and texture. Once they are fully dried, they can be kept unrefrigerated for long periods. Some dried sausages are also fermented, either with naturally occurring organisms or by adding a starter (such as *Lactobacillus*) to the forcemeat. Such fermentation produces lactic acid, which preserves the meat ('cooking' it, in much the same way as lime juice denatures the fish protein in ceviche) and also creates a range of tangy flavouring compounds. *Landjäger*, *soppressata* and some kinds of chorizo are fermented. Many sausages are smoked, either while fresh or after some time spent hanging in cool air to cure. Smoking is done for two reasons: to help prevent the meat from spoiling and to add flavour.

Sausages are prominent in cuisines from all parts of the globe, despite the development of newer, technological means of preserving meats. Many peasant cultures have enhanced their largely vegetarian diets with small quantities of highly seasoned sausage. Not only does the sausage taste good, but it makes use of scraps and other unsaleable meats that would otherwise go to waste. In more modern and upscale cuisines, sausages make up for their high fat and sodium content by contributing greater flavour and variety than their size would suggest. They can therefore satisfy sophisticated palates, using lower quantities of protein and fat, while providing a spectrum of culinary pleasures that range from rustic to elegant.

Sausage cookery – like many of the world's great cuisines – may have begun as peasant food, but it has risen to the heights of gastronomic bliss. That is not to say, however, that we have forgotten its humble beginnings. Many sausage jokes play on the taint of residual crudeness – of class and/or ingredients. Bismarck's alleged famous comparison between the sleaziness of legislation and the metamorphosis of mystery meat comes to mind. The French prime minister Édouard Marie Herriot, in the years before the Second World War, said much the same thing, but with Gallic flair: 'Politics is like an *andouillette* – it should smell a little like shit, but not too much.' Another

Sausages have long been the butt of low humour . . . and many believe puns like this to be the lowest. This postcard dates from 1907.

politician, Mitt Romney, while on the campaign trail for the American presidency, quipped: 'A waitress told me once that scrapple is "what doesn't make it into the sausage". And I was like, there's stuff that doesn't qualify for the sausage?'[3]

None of these defamatory remarks were new. Sausages have provided a hook on which to hang jokes at least as far back as Aristophanes in the fifth century BC. In *The Knights*, the lowly sausage-seller Agoracritus is accosted by Demosthenes and Cleon in the *agora*. Agoracritus wants to be left alone to wash his tripe and sell his sausages, but Demosthenes has other plans for him, this 'sad rascal without shame, no better than a common market rogue'. He lists Agoracritus' qualifications for success in politics:

> Continue your trade. Mix and knead together all the state business as you do for your sausages. To win the people, always cook them some savoury that pleases them. Besides, you possess all the attributes of a demagogue; a screeching, horrible voice, a perverse, cross-grained nature and the language of the marketplace. In you all is united that is needful for governing. The oracles are in your favour, even including that of Delphi. Come, take a chaplet, offer a libation to the god of Stupidity and take care to fight vigorously.

After a long argument with the politician, replete with dozens of sausage-based double entendres, Agoracritus wallops Cleon with a sausage. A much later story – Guy de Maupassant's nineteenth-century 'A Vendetta' – features a sausage used as a weapon in another way. A woman trains her dog to attack the neck of her enemy by fashioning a dummy from old clothes, with a sausage for a necktie. She starves the dog until it is frantic, then releases it to gobble the sausage. She repeats this for three months, until the dog is taken to see her enemy, with predictable results. (The same strategy figures largely in *Hannibal* by Thomas Harris, substituting vicious pigs for the family dog.)

There is one sausage joke in the *Philogelos*, the oldest surviving collection of jokes: 'A cook with halitosis is frying a sausage. But he breathes on it so much that he turns it into a turd.' Today, the joke is likely only to amuse an audience of eight-year-olds.

Book 9 of Athenaeus' *The Deipnosophists* (early third century AD) features a discussion of ham and the mustard that accompanies it, and quotes Epicharmus' *Kyklops* (*The Cyclops*), which dates from the fifth century BC: 'Sausages are nice, I swear by Zeus, and so is a ham [*koleos*].' Athenaeus continues: 'Learn this, too, of me, most learned men, that in this line Epicharmus speaks of sausage as *chordé*, though elsewhere he always calls it *orya*.' The mention of *orya* is significant because Epicharmus, the earliest known writer of Greek comedies, wrote an entire comedy called *Orya* (*The Sausage*) in about 500 BC, almost a century before Aristophanes' *The Knights*. It no longer exists, except in small fragments, but there is a lot of speculation that it played largely upon the phallic appearance of sausages. Epicharmus was not only recognized by Socrates, Plato and Theocritus as Greece's greatest comic writer, but was also a philosopher and follower of Pythagoras – so, ironically, he was probably a vegetarian.

Visual puns associated with sausage are frequent; think of 'hot dog' or 'weiner dog' for frankfurters, or the Italian *coglioni di mulo* (mule's balls) from Campotosto. The latter are not actually made from the family jewels of mules, but take their name from their dangling, bulbous shape. *Culatello* takes its name from the Italian slang for 'anus', in which its forcemeat is cured.

Hot dogs and other sausages (for obvious reasons) are slang words for penis, as in the game of 'hide the sausage', or, in the North American version, 'hide the salami' or 'hide the baloney'. These are ancient jokes, going back at least to Epicharmus, and probably earlier. Sausages were even part of Roman fertility rites, which led to them being banned briefly by Constantine the Great in the fourth century AD. Like the American experiment with Prohibition centuries later, the ban only created a thriving black market, and it too was repealed after a few years.

Sausages have always had a coarse and slightly ridiculous aspect, and one saint played on that for effect. In sixth-century Syria, St Simeon Salos earned a reputation as the patron saint of fools. While he did many good deeds in secret, he feigned lunacy when anyone was watching. He claimed that he acted in this way to achieve *apathea*, a state that marked him as an outcast, in order to be more perfectly penitent. Among his 'foolish' acts were eating sausages on the steps of the church on Good Friday, and walking around town dragging a dead dog while wearing a necklace of sausages.

The crude English slang 'get stuffed' may not refer literally to sausage, but it is certainly not far from the 'meat' of the subject. Blues lyrics are replete with food-based sexual euphemisms, and we can be sure that no one was confused when Bessie Smith sang about needing 'a hot dog in my roll'. In a twist on the old 'Why buy a cow when you can get milk for free?' comment, a common joke has it that 'nowadays, 80 per cent of women are against marriage . . . because they realize it's not worth buying an entire pig just to get a little sausage.'

On the subject of little sausages, John Waters's film *Pink Flamingos* (1972) transports – as Waters so often does – the merely obscene to the frontiers of the ridiculous, and beyond. One character, the polymorphously perverse Raymond Marble, exposes himself in a park – but, when his trench coat opens, we discover a large salami suspended from his genitalia.

In December 2011, when Martha Stewart was making a television segment about homemade sausage, she noticed that hog casings resembled condoms. Not knowing when to abandon an embarrassing moment on camera (and microphone), she continued by opining that they would work, as they were 'good enough for sausage'. She has since made sure that the video has been removed from the Internet.

It is obvious that sausage jokes are rarely sophisticated, and some of the least tolerable (but still funny) ones are puns. German ones are consistently the *Wurst*. For example, this sign

FRESH SAUSAGES

Hush, little doggie, | You'll be a Wienerwurst,
Don't you cry, | Bye and bye.

698/34

All sausages, not just hot dogs, have been suspected of containing
'mystery meats'. This card is undated, but the stamp on the reverse
suggests it was posted between 1908 and 1909.

has probably appeared in many butcher shop windows: 'Our Wurst is our Best – You can't beat our Meat.'

'Phoney-baloney', which seems to have appeared in American slang in the late nineteenth century (and was common in the first decades of the twentieth), did not refer to substandard bologna, an Americanized version of morta-della (nor did P. G. Wodehouse's – and Damon Runyon's – mock-Latin 'phonus balonus'). It merely added a rhyming word for emphasis. 'Phoney' seems to have been based, in turn, on 'fawney', British underworld slang for a kind of con game.[4] However, 'baloney' was a common term for bologna in the USA at the time, and was used in the same conning sense: 'The sausage origin has merit, on the analogy that it's a mixture of ground-up meat and then you stuff the casing. Hence, mix up a tale and stuff the auditor.'[5]

The mystery-meat aspect of sausages has led to a great deal of suspicion over the years about their role in a healthy diet. Today's bête noire is fat – and sausage's fat content is no secret

A British postcard, printed soon after the publication in 1906 of Upton Sinclair's muck-raking book *The Jungle*.

(a lean sausage is a dry, unappetizing one). However, in the early years of the twentieth century, Upton Sinclair's book *The Jungle* focused American attention on sanitation and food safety. Popular disgust forced the creation of food-safety laws and bureaucracies to enforce them. Two decades earlier, in Victorian England, similar concerns about the healthiness (or lack thereof) of sausages begat a crusade against those, especially fresh ones, which were suspected of causing a rash of food poisoning among the poor. While sanitation and social justice were the problems in post-Sinclair America, 'irritant poisoning' – adulteration – was the culprit in England.

Despite being the subject of so much low humour, and some justifiable fear, sausages continue to be among the most popular foodstuffs (or stuffed foods). A survey conducted in 2011 by Harris Interactive for the National Hot Dog and Sausage Council in the USA found that

> More than four in five U.S. adults (82 per cent) eat sausage . . . This includes 87 per cent of men and 77 per cent of women . . . When asked at which meal they most often eat sausage, the majority of adults (54 per cent) said they most often eat sausage at breakfast, compared to 26 per cent at dinner and 4 per cent at lunch. More women than men, 30 per cent to 21 per cent, respectively, said they most often eat sausage at dinner.[6]

The survey did not even address the consumption of hot dogs – which, for many Americans, are so huge a part of their culinary culture that they are not even considered part of the larger category 'sausages'. The writer H. L. Mencken grew up loving the American wiener, but later complained that 'they contained precisely the same rubber, indigestible pseudo-sausages that millions of Americans now eat'.[7] Still later, after his wife died (and with her, his source of good home-cooked food), he reverted to his earlier hot-dog diet.

But it is not just frankfurters on the grill, in a stadium or covered with curry-flavoured ketchup on a Berlin *Strasse*. Sausages are a big part of a global renaissance of artisanal charcuterie. The chef George Marsh of Woodberry Kitchen in Baltimore is thrilled to be rediscovering – and reimagining – some of these ancient culinary arts:

> When you get a whole, entire animal, there's a lot of stuff that you need to learn how to use. Not only is it a fun, exciting thing to do – and dried and cured meats are delicious – but we wanted to create products using pastured, locally raised animals.

Hog liver goes into pâté, and heads and trotters are made into scrapple. Marsh also roasts whole heads and makes blood sausage.[8] He is part of a trend that is linked to the Slow Food movement, but is also connected to an urge to show respect for the animals we eat, and a desire to explore the taste of history that would otherwise be lost. In a similar vein, the English chef Fergus Henderson's nose-to-tail approach to cooking (using parts of animals that would otherwise be wasted) has revived the kind of frugality that led to the invention of sausages. The writer John Barlow has addressed the same waste-not-want-not attitude in his book *Everything but the Squeal: Eating the Whole Hog in Northern Spain* (2008).

Along the way, cooks like Barlow, Henderson and Marsh have learned what our ancestors already knew: the 'mystery meats' in sausages can provide some delicious surprises.

2
Some Historical Sausages and the Links Between Them

All sausages begin their lives as fresh sausagemeat. No matter how they are processed after that, they begin as some form of protein that is cut, chopped, minced or pounded, then combined with salt and – usually – some other form of seasoning. Fresh sausage may be formed into patties, stuffed into casings or even used loose, crumbled into sauces or as a garnish for poultry stuffing, like American breakfast sausage.

Fresh sausages must be cooked before they can be consumed. Modern pig farming has largely eliminated the risk of trichinosis; the only u.s. cases reported in recent years came from eating bear meat. The parasites can be spread only by eating the flesh of other flesh-eating mammals, and modern pigs live almost entirely on vegetable matter. However, all sorts of bacterial and parasitical disease can result from consuming raw, uncured sausage. This applies to sausages made from flesh other than pork, too: raw beef, poultry and some seafood can contain harmful pathogens. Good cooks always 'taste as they go', but when making sausage, it is important to fry any samples to check for seasoning before stuffing an entire batch into casings.

Variations on the fresh sausage theme can be found everywhere, from the *julkorv* of Sweden to the *boerewors* of South

Africa, from the *si-klok* of Thailand to the *Haagse leverworst* of the Netherlands. Fresh sausage, before the age of artificial refrigeration, had a short shelf life before spoilage – decomposition – set in. Salt helped, of course, in preserving the meat, but unless the salt content was so high that the sausage had to be soaked in fresh water before becoming palatable (like some hams, and salt cod, today), another method was required for long-term storage.

The primary cause of meat spoilage is bacteria. These bacteria could have been present in the meat all along, but held to manageable levels by the animal's immune system (which ceases to be in effect once the animal is slaughtered). Bacteria can also find their way into the meat from environmental sources, notably cross-contamination during processing, via insects or simply through the air.

Sometimes the bacteria can harm us directly, by causing infection, but more commonly the waste products they create (while digesting the meat we are trying to preserve for

Demonstrating how to fill *boudin blanc* at Le Cordon Bleu.

ourselves) make us ill through intoxication. Unfortunately, not all forms of intoxication are recreational; no one chooses food poisoning for the fun of it.

Bacteria require food (the meat), water and the proper temperature in order to prosper. Two of the simpler strategies for discouraging the growth of harmful bacteria involve reducing moisture to levels where they cannot live and lowering temperature to a point at which their reproduction rate is kept to a minimum. Methods used to control bacteria, whether harmful or beneficial, are discussed under 'Curing' in chapter Five.

Our ancestors also learned, early on, that hanging meat near a smoky fire helped it to resist spoilage. Smoked sausages, as well as hams and jerky, benefit from the treatment in several ways. First, the length of the drying period is reduced, giving 'bad' bacteria less time to do their nasty business. Second, the smoke creates an impenetrable barrier, making later contamination less likely. Third, many of the compounds in the smoke possess anti-microbial properties. Best of all, the smoke creates flavours that *we* find very attractive.

Aside from pork's gastronomic qualities, pigs are efficient converters of foods that humans do not want for themselves (waste scraps and 'mast' – the acorns and such that pigs can find for themselves in the forest). As long as there is adequate water (pigs need it – or mud – to keep themselves cool), they are an economical source of human food. Hot, dry places, such as the Middle East, do not provide ideal porcine environments, which may explain why Jews and Muslims have long anathematized the pig. Regions that are not suitable for raising pigs have developed sausage cuisines based on whatever animal protein is available; as we shall see later, everything from reindeer to kangaroo has found its way into sausage casings.

As humans have dispersed around the globe, they have taken favourite food traditions with them, and assimilated new ingredients and processes wherever they found them. The range of seasonings we use in all our cooking, including the production of sausage, reflects the history of trade and the migration of populations around the globe.

According to some rather questionable food history, perhaps better known as 'fakelore', sausages were invented by the Roman emperor Nero's chef in the middle of the first century AD. Since they were mentioned almost 1,000 years earlier, in the *Odyssey*, Nero's chef appears not to have been much of an innovator.

In fact, despite commercial hype and self-promotion, new dishes are rarely 'invented'. Cooks usually refine or modify older recipes, or combine aspects of other known dishes or cuisines in new ways. So Nero's chef *might* have developed a new variation on the sausage theme, just as many others have done, before and after him.

Sausages were known, generically, to ancient Romans as *farvimen*, a word that is the source of our culinary term *farci*, 'stuffed'. Other names for sausage included *circelli, insicia* (or *incisia*), *lucanica* and *tomacinae. Insicia* appear often in the Roman recipe collection *De re coquinaria* (known most commonly by the name of its alleged author, the fifth-century Apicius, though the book was actually assembled centuries after his death from a number of sources), usually in minced seafood sausages that are the ancestors of our quenelles. The first-century Roman poet Martial described the steaming *tomacinae* sold by the raucous street vendors of Rome: the aptly named *pendulus* was large (filling the caecum, or intestine, of a pig), and was served in slices; another favourite street food of the time, the *botulus*, was a thick blood sausage. *Botulus* comes down to us in the names for the Spanish sausages *botillo* and *butiellu*, and one from Portugal, *botelo*. The names are all ultimately derived from the Latin word for 'intestine', *botellus*.

In the *Satyricon* of Petronius Arbiter, a first-century Roman courtier, the wealthy (but utterly inept) poet Trimalchio gives a feast at which an immense wild boar is brought before the guests. Trimalchio pretends to be upset that his cook has neglected to gut the animal before cooking it. The beast is hacked open and a mass of sausages spills out – stuffed entrails posing as entrails – to everyone's delight. This Roman joke (known as *Porcus Troianus*, literally 'Trojan pig') was also mentioned in the early fifth-century *Saturnalia convivia* by Macrobius, who claimed it was well known two centuries before Petronius.

Sausage recipes are plentiful in *De re coquinaria* in the fourth to fifth centuries. Apicius was a famous gourmet who, legend has it, committed suicide when he feared he would no longer be able to feed his patrician tastes in the manner to which they had become accustomed. His 'bank account'

Assorted sausages and pâtés on sale in Paris.

Charcutería in Barcelona.

had fallen to the equivalent of a few million of today's pounds. *De re coquinaria* was clearly intended to provide delicacies for diners with discriminating palates. Sausages may have begun in frugality but, by classical times, they had already evolved into viands worthy of a gourmet's attention.

Book Two of *De re coquinaria* begins with a series of forcemeats: mixed shellfish with cumin, lovage, pepper and *silphium* (a foul-smelling resin made from the sap of a plant that was harvested to extinction in Nero's day); squid beaten to a paste with liquamen (a Roman staple similar to the salty fish sauce *nam pla*); prawns or crayfish pounded with liquamen and pepper; roasted pork liver minced with liquamen, rue and pepper, wrapped in bay leaves and smoked; cooked brains pounded until as smooth as *mortadella*, with liquamen, lovage, oregano and pepper, then bound with eggs; cooked mussels pounded to a paste with *alica* (a semolina-like grain), liquamen and pepper (the forcemeat was then studded with pine nuts

31

David Hopfer (1493–1536), *The Sausage Seller and the Carnival Dancers*, etching and engraving.

and peppercorns, wrapped in caul fat and roasted); unspecified meat pounded with pepper and liquamen, bound with bread-crumbs and wine, then finished as with the mussel forcemeat above; and finally another unidentified forcemeat seasoned with camomile, liquamen, lovage and pepper.

Apicius even rated the different sausage meats, after specifying that they be 'fried until they burst their skins'. His favourite was peacock, followed by pheasant, rabbit and chicken. Pork, the most familiar sausage meat today, came in last. He included in his collection a couple of variations on black pudding, or blood sausage. One combined blood with chopped pine nuts and leeks, pepper and hard-boiled egg yolks. They were stuffed into casings and poached in a bath of liquamen and wine. Another contained fat, leeks, liquamen, lovage, pepper and raw egg, garnished with peppercorns and pine nuts.

Today's Greek *loukanika* and Italian *luganega* are etymo-logical descendants of a sausage that first appeared in writing in Latin (*De re coquinaria*) and in Greek papyri, both in the fourth century. The Greek *loukánikon* and Roman *lucanicae* take their name from Lucania, part of Magna Graecia in southern Italy (Paestum, just south of the Amalfi coast, has a better-preserved Greek temple than any in Greece). Roman soldiers encountered these sausages when they conquered the region in the second century and, like the GIs of the Second World War, brought home a taste for foreign food. Apicius mentions *lucanicae* some eleven times, with recipes calling for berries – not leaves – of bay, cumin, parsley, pepper, rue and savory. The required measure of salt was provided by liquamen. Again, the forcemeat was pounded in a mortar to a smooth paste, then a garnish of fat, whole peppercorns and pine nuts was added. The mixture was forced into casings and hung in smoke. It is difficult to know precisely what the original *lucanicae* were like, since no meat was specified and no measurements were provided.

In present-day Greece, however, *loukanika* (or *loukaniko*) is made from minced pork and lamb, seasoned with fennel seeds and orange zest and stuffed into hog casings. In addition to the above, local Greek variants might contain coriander, garlic, oregano, pepper and/or thyme, and some Greeks marinate the sausages in wine before grilling them. They are served either as meze (appetizers) or as part of a main course. While the Romans preferred their sausage smoked, most Greek versions are consumed fresh.

With the fall of Rome, and the end of the classical age, literary references to sausage nearly disappear. This is not a sign that sausages were not being eaten, of course, just that people were not writing about them. In fact, after several plagues ravaged Europe, a lot of farmland reverted to forest, and oak and beech woodland meant good foraging for pigs. It is very likely that those reduced human populations actually ate more pork.

In Europe, literacy was largely restricted to the clergy. While monks were very good at copying the works of the ancients (at least if they supported Christian orthodoxy), they were not interested in writing anything as frivolous as cookbooks. However, the Islamic world was experiencing a literary flowering of its own. Islamic scholars were carefully preserving the Greek, Roman and Hebrew texts from which Europe's Renaissance would later spring, and writing about the arts, including the culinary arts. Two inhabitants of what is now Iraq – Ibn Sayyar al-Warraq, writing in the tenth century, and Muhammad bin Hasan al-Baghdadi in the thirteenth – wrote books with the same title: *Kitab al-Tabikh* (The Book of Dishes). In fact, these books were not written but rather compiled, much as was *De re coquinaria*. The earlier *Kitab al-Tabikh* contained recipes for *masir* (a kind of sausage, stuffed into sheep intestines, that is still made today); a lamb's-liver sausage wrapped in caul fat; and *laqaniq* (once again, there's that etymological connection to *lucanica*). For religious reasons, sausages were made with chicken, goat and lamb, but they were flavoured with a host of ingredients: herbs such as coriander, rue, spikenard and thyme, and many spices from southern Asia, including cassia, cloves, galangal, ginger and pepper. The later volume adds a sausage called *sukhtur* that was bulked out with rice and chickpeas, and contained the additional flavours of cinnamon, cumin, mastic and saffron.

The High Middle Ages brought a flowering of courtly life, and with it a kind of conspicuous consumption that had not been seen in Europe for centuries. After the Crusades re-introduced Europe to the kind of spices (and literature) that had been known to the ancients – and were still known in the Islamic Middle East – the diet of Europe changed. Just as today, consumption (at least among the well-off) reflected the medical beliefs of the time, and the nobility used expensive foods to show off their wealth and health-consciousness. Today we are concerned about fat and carbohydrates, because that is what our doctors tell us, based on today's science. In the Middle Ages, doctors followed the writings of Avicenna (Ibn Sīnā, a tenth-century Persian), and the food they consumed had a distinctly Middle Eastern flavour. They used lots of spices, and even their 'savoury' dishes contained fruit and sugar. Some of those flavour profiles are still seen in some of today's most old-fashioned sausages and puddings.

The demand for foreign luxuries, such as spices and sugar, led to an attempt to bypass the Middle Eastern merchants who maintained a monopoly on the spice trade. This led to the Age of Exploration, which coincided with the Renaissance – a period in which Europe literally and figuratively expanded its horizons. For our purposes, that expansion had several effects. Finding new routes and cheaper supplies of sugar and spice meant that these commodities were no longer as luxurious as they had been, and their appeal to conspicuous consumers was reduced. The rediscovery of the works of the second-century Greek doctor and philosopher Galen meant that the medical beliefs of the period moved away from Middle Eastern influences. Both factors caused a change in taste, and the highly seasoned and perfumed foods of the past fell out of favour.

The new flowering of literacy and the arts meant that cookbooks began to be written again (and, a little later, printed), so we can see the culinary changes reflected in the variety and distribution of sausages. While some well-known fourteenth-century cookbooks (the English *The Forme of Cury*, or Forms of Cooking, and German *Das Buch von Guter Spise*, or Book of Good Food) do not specifically mention sausages, others do. The anonymous *Ménagier de Paris* (The Goodman of Paris), written in the last decade of the century, includes *boudins* made of blood, goose or liver; *andouilles*; and a pork sausage made with fennel. The late fourteenth-century *Libro di Cucina*, or Kitchen Book, by an anonymous Venetian, gives recipes for *mortadella* (a version made of liver, eggs and cheese); a 'smoked yellow sausage' with a casing marinated in white wine and saffron; and a grilled liver sausage, *fegatelli*, wrapped in caul fat. Many of the recipes call for *poudre fort* (a mixture of cinnamon, cloves, ginger, mace, pepper and cubebs – tailed pepper, *Piper cubeba*), a common medieval ingredient. Today's *quatre épices* is a descendant of both *poudre fort* and the similar *poudre douce* (cinnamon, cloves, ginger and nutmeg). In the U.S., pumpkin-pie spice blends can also be traced to these medieval mixtures.

By the fifteenth century, cookbooks had grown fat with sausage recipes. *Libro della cocina*, by an anonymous Tuscan, had *mortadella* and *comandella* filled with fish, chopped cooked greens and onions; *florio*, a hard, dry salame; an unnamed sausage filled with cooked calf's stomach, eggs and cheese; other unnamed sausages of pork or veal with herbs; *tomacelli*; and another *mortadella*, made with pork liver, marjoram, pepper, saffron and wine.

Maestro Martino's *Libro de arte coquinaria* (Book of the Art of Cooking) shows the influence of cooking in northern Italy (near Milan and Como), as well as that of Naples. Many of his recipes ended up in *De honesta voluptate et valetudine* (On Honourable Pleasure and Health), by his friend and admirer Platina (Bartolomeo Sacchi). These books included recipes for veal *mortadella*, *tomacelli* of liver or pork belly and cheese, a yellow *cervellata* of pork or veal, and a pork-and-fennel sausage that resembles Italian sausages, based on *lucanicae*, still made today. Platina's *lucanicae* were hung in smoke.

The *Cuoco napoletano*, or Neapolitan Cook, was not published in the fifteenth century, but was assembled from items in a manuscript from that period (now in New York's Morgan

Library). Its recipe for *tomaselle* includes liver and of pork belly with eggs, young and aged cheeses, raisins, herbs and spices, wrapped in caul fat and fried in lard. An unnamed sausage consists of walnuts, cheese, garlic, raisins, spices and veal fat stuffed into calf intestine. The *cirvelato* is a boiled sausage of veal or pork with eggs, cheese (specifically Parmigiano) and spices. The inclusion of eggs and cheese in so many of these recipes is unusual, but there are also instructions for making 'good' or 'Bolognese' sausage, which contained only pork (or veal), pepper and more salt than other sausages.

At the beginning of the sixteenth century, an anonymous author published *Manual de mujeres en el cual se contienen muchas y diversas recetas muy buenas* (Manual for Women in which is Contained Many and Diverse Very Good Recipes). It is fascinating to see a recipe for chorizo from a period just before chillies from the New World became an essential ingredient. The sausage combined pork flesh and fat with ground cloves, garlic, salt and white wine, bulked out with flour. The forcemeat was left to mature for a day before stuffing, and was then hung in smoke. The *Manual de mujeres* contains two blood sausages (*morcilla*): one is bound with breadcrumbs, seasoned with cinnamon and cloves, and garnished with almonds, pine nuts and cooked egg yolks, while in the other, pork is added.

Livre fort excellent de cuysine (The Most Excellent Book of Cookery), published in the mid-sixteenth century, marks the transition between the cooking of the Renaissance and the recognizable French cookery that appears first in La Varenne's *Le Cuisinier françois*, a century later. Its recipe for *andouille* (whether made from pork, veal or mutton offal) had the saffron-stained casings we saw in Platina and the *Libro di cucina*, but the saffron was dissolved in tangy verjuice instead of wine – and the sausage was cold-smoked in the chimney. Several types of *boudin* are included: one with veal or mutton livers, garnished with onion, gooseberries or sour grapes; white *boudins* of veal or pork with goose fat, milk and egg yolk; and another with fat and cooked pork liver, seasoned with herbs, again garnished with gooseberries or sour grapes. Its bologna is nothing but pork, beef and pork fat (in equal parts), plus salt and whole peppercorns. It also contains a recipe for *cervelat*, and something called Lombard sausage, a smoked mixture of capons and such game birds as snipe and partridge.

Cervelat appears as *Zervelat* in *Das Kochbuch der Sabina Welserin* (The Cookbook of Sabina Welserin, 1553), a very early German cookbook, and one of the first written in any language by a woman. It contains a piece of advice about stuffing sausages not found in today's cookery manuals: 'This should be done during the crescent moon.' Welserin's yellow *Zervelats* were sweetly spiced with cinnamon, cloves, nutmeg and sugar. Like every German sausage book since then, *Das Kochbuch* included recipes for *Bratwurst*, *Liverwurst* (although most others do not include pigs' lungs, caraway seeds and diced bacon, as here) and venison sausage. The last recipe made use of the deer's liver, lungs and fat, whereas most modern venison sausages contain milder-tasting pork fat.

Cristoforo di Messibugo, writing before the mid-sixteenth century (he died in 1548, but his *Banchetti, composizioni di vivande e apparecchio generale* did not come out until 1549), outlined everything one needed to know about preparing and serving a noble banquet. Less well-known is his *Libro novo a far d'ogni sorte di vivanda* (A New Book, in which All Types of Food are Taught, 1557), which included some twenty sausage recipes. He provided directions for many of the sausages we have already seen: several different *mortadelle*; multiple liver sausages (*tomaselle*); *zambudelli*, made with offal, like *andouillettes*; red, white, 'Ducal' and French *cervellati* – red with blood, white

David Teniers the Younger, *Sausage-making*, 1651.

with cheese, egg whites and milk in place of meat, 'Ducal' with livers and saffron, and French with veal and fennel.

Bartolomeo Scappi's monumental *Opera dell'arte del cucinare* (Complete Art of Cooking, 1570) contained close to 1,000 recipes. It was very influential, being translated into both Dutch and Spanish. Scappi provided instructions for the butchering and preservation of meats (hams, game birds and fats, as well as sausages), and for recognizing spoilage. His recipes are distinguished from their predecessors by their careful attention to the details of every step of their preparation. Sausages for which he gives instructions include *tommacelle*; saveloys, with and without sweetbreads; *mortadelle*; blood sausages; forcemeats of all kinds from different meats, fruits, truffles, nuts and cheeses; and various fish sausages made from pike, sturgeon, trout and tuna.

Lancelot de Casteau's *Ouverture de cuisine* (Opening the Kitchen, 1604) also features a number of fish sausages. His *sausisse de Bologne de poisson* in no way resembles anything we might recognize as bologna; it is made from carp and fresh and smoked salmon, with wine, cinnamon and eggs. Casteau also offered two recipes for sausages made from sturgeon, one from pike and even one from dogfish (a small shark).

The *New Kochbuch* of Marx Rumpolt (1581) contains some unusual sausages: one of mutton and bacon, enclosed in sheep's caul fat; *Hirnwürst*, a poached brain sausage made with eggs, ginger, pepper and saffron; several different ways to stuff a pig's stomach; some sausages that are clearly antecedents of modern German sausages; and a brief allusion to a supposedly Italian beef sausage called *Zurwonada*. This large cold-smoked sausage, Rumpolt assured his readers, was 'a good dish . . . for a poor fellow and also for a great lord'. The *Kunstbuch Von Mancherley Essen* (1598) by Frantz de Rontzier provided instructions '*von mancherley Würsten und zum Ersten von Zozissen Würste zumachen*' (on many *Wursts* and firstly on making sausage *Wursts*). Some are what modern Germans would call *Kochwurst* – that is, they are made from pre-cooked meats. For example, *klein Zozischen* (small sausages) contained roasted pork flesh, kidneys and bacon. The book also supplies several recipes for game sausages, using hare, venison and wild boar.

Some British cookbooks from the end of the century, such as *A Book of Cookrye Very Necessary for All Such as Delight Therein* (1587), still favoured the sweet and complex spice mixtures of the Middle Ages. Two different liver sausages call for cloves, dates, mace, raisins, saffron and sugar. Clearly, the distinction between sweets and savouries was not yet established in the English palate.

The ancient *lucanicae* of Rome must have existed during the dark ages of cookbooks (the period between the fall of Rome and the resurgence of food publishing that we have described), because they have a host of descendants in far-flung locations around the world. The sausage – or, at least, its name – has travelled all over Europe, and on to many of the places Europeans colonized. Descendants of the Roman sausages still exist in many parts of Italy. Basilicata has its *lucanica*, Lombardy its *luganiga*, Veneto its *luganega di Treviso*, Piedmont its *luganeghin* and Corsica its *lonzo*.

In Portugal, *linguiça*, the etymological descendant of *lucanica*, is garlicky and red from paprika (obviously not an ingredient the Romans would have known, evidence that the recipe continued to evolve after the discovery of the New World). A fondness for *linguiça* accompanied colonists from Portugal to Angola and Brazil, where it continued to evolve in response to local taste and ingredients. In Mangalore, once a Portuguese port on India's Arabian Sea coast, there is still a Roman Catholic populace. Their *linguiça* takes on a slightly South Asian flavour, with hotter chillies and a little turmeric.

The Spanish chorizo and its Portuguese relation, *chouriço*, both became completely different sausages after the New World supplied chillies. They continued to evolve – some losing contact with their European roots, others maintaining them – resulting in the wide range of Mexican and other Latin American chorizos we know today.

3
Sausages of Europe

Although sausages are prepared all over the world, some regions have produced a greater diversity of types than others. Europeans have been by far the most prolific, possibly as a result of having an ideal environment for raising pigs, good supplies of salt and a seasonally cool climate for curing hams and sausages. The sausage traditions that might immediately spring to mind – English, French, German and Italian – are not the only ones in Europe, however; in fact, the European Union has granted special recognition to other regional sausages in the form of Certificates of Origin. This designation is meant to safeguard the products' names, much as the French *Appelation d'Origine Contrôlée* (AOC) protects the 'brand names' of special wines. Since the earliest known sausages come from the Mediterranean region, we will begin with the descendants of ancient Rome (many more regional sausages are listed in the Appendix).

Italy

It is important to remember that Italy has been unified for only about a century and a half. While its culinary roots are

Die Fette Küche by Pieter Bruegel, 16th century. Note that the only slender person pictured is the musician who is being shoved, selfishly, out of the door.

Roman – and possibly Etruscan – for most of its history Italy was gaggle of warring city-states. The poet Dante, writing at the end of the thirteenth and beginning of the fourteenth centuries, tried to create a unified Italian language. Seven centuries later, despite a national language being legally defined, regional linguistic differences still survive – and culinary xenophobia keeps local sausage variations as independent as the local tongue.

Some sausage types are found almost everywhere in Italy: *cacciatore* and *cacciatorini* (small dried sausages, ideal for carrying in a hunter's pocket) can be found in seven provinces; *capocollo* (the name comes from the part of the pig used: the 'cape', or back of the neck to the shoulder blades; the meat in large chunks, not minced), *cotechino* (fresh sausage that must be cooked before serving) and *soppressata* (pressed sausage) in at least four. However, most Italians consider food from the next

Still-life with Grapes, Sausages, Cucumber, Bread and a Bird, oil by an unknown Italian master, 17th century.

town to be 'foreign', and so the concept of 'Italian food' is meaningless in Italy.

There may be hundreds of regional varieties of salami. Most are dried (*salame di San Benedetto Po* is cured *sotto la cenere*, 'under the ashes') and fermented sausages that can be stored, unrefrigerated, for a decade. The Italian climate – warm, dry and breezy – is perfect for the production of dry-cured sausages. Most are raw but cured, allowing them to be eaten as they are, although Piedmontese *salame cotto* is cooked, as its name indicates. Most contain garlic and are made from pork, although beef, goose, turkey, venison and even horse are used as well. Salami is made everywhere in the world today, but especially in Europe – and Italians make more varieties than anyone else. The word itself is Italian, and refers to salt, via the Latin *sal*, a nod to Italy's Roman past. *Salami* is the plural

Classic New Year's pairing of *cotechino* sausage and lentils, as served in Modena.

Italian cured salame, with white *Penicillium* mould.

of *salame*; *salumi* is a broader term, encompassing all cured meats; and a *salumeria* is a shop that makes and/or sells *salumi*.

France

Like other regions once 'visited' by Roman legions, France (then Gaul) has a strong sausage tradition. It is not always easy to tell in which direction the recipes travelled, though; for example, one type of blood sausage can be found, under different names, across a geographical band of Roman occupation: it might be called *botifarra negra* in Catalan-speaking regions of Spain; *morcilla* elsewhere in Spain, Andorra and France; *saucisson d'oc* in Provence (a region of France that is still littered with Roman architecture); or *mustardela* in the Valdesi valley of northern Italy.

Unlike the Italians, whose gastronomy, language and culture are fragmented and fiercely regional, the French have

Botifarras soledeñas.

Le Gourmand, illustration from J. F Goez's *Exercises d'imagination de differens caractères et formes humaines, inventés peints et dessinés* (1784).

more of a national persona (with the possible exception of those from Languedoc, the very name of which acknowledges the local Provençal language). When the Romans arrived, the locals already had a number of sausages that resemble those that are still made there. The fourteenth-century household guide *Le Ménagier de Paris* contained detailed instructions for the preparation of sausages and puddings that used virtually all parts of the pig's anatomy.

A *saucisson* is a large sausage, while *saucisse* is the diminutive. A *cochon* is a pig, but a *cochonnaille* is a platter of *saucissons*,

Charcuterie in Paris with large pâtés.

saucisses and assorted other charcuterie – a French pork-lover's version of antipasto.

The French borrow ingredients and cooking techniques from all over the world, somehow making the resulting dishes more French than their names might suggest. The only thing Spanish about a *saucisse Espagnole* is the tiny amount of sweet or hot paprika in the recipe; the *quatre épices* and garnish of raisins are hardly traditional on the south side of the Pyrenees.

French charcuteries are likely to carry sausages from all over the country, and even – *sacre bleu!* – from non-Gallic sources. So, rather than divide the sausages geographically, we will sort these French examples by type, although there is often overlap between some of the categories.

The most basic French sausages are uncured, and sold fresh or raw. *Andouilles* contain tripe. *Caillettes*, *crépinettes* and *gayettes* are fresh sausages wrapped in caul fat. The sweet-savoury *saucisse de Toulouse* – containing cayenne, black and white pepper, nutmeg and sugar – is usually stuffed and coiled into one continuous sausage, held flat with a couple of crossed skewers ready for grilling. The forcemeat also fills any voids when fabricating galantines of boned poultry.

Saucissons à cuire are cooked as part of the sausage-making process, unlike the fresh ones that are cooked later at home. *Boudin* is generic French for any sausage, or, for that matter, any food in the form of a sausage; the English word 'pudding' is derived from it. *Boudin noir* is a black pudding, while *boudin blanc* gets its pale colour from chicken, turkey or veal plus cream. *Saucisse aux fruits de mer* is a seafood-lover's dream, filled with a mousse of scallops, prawns and white fish, heady with vermouth. Garlic and a garnish of pistachios give *saucisson à l'ail aux pistaches* its name. *Saucisson cuit au Madère* is a cooked sausage flavoured with Madeira and *quatre épices*, garnished

Pure pork sausages, market day in Foix, France.

with truffles and pistachios. It is uncured (so cannot be eaten raw), but rests for a couple of days to allow the flavours to mature.

Cured or dried sausages are known as *saucisses sèches* or *saucissons secs*. The term *cervelas* referred originally to sausages containing brains, then to cured pork sausages, redolent of garlic, but can now also be applied to delicate, unsmoked sausages made with seafood. *Cervelas de Lyon* can be garnished with any number of expensive ingredients, from truffles to morels. While *cervelas* is related to the *Cervelat* of Germany, it is descended more directly from a Florentine sausage.

Smoked sausages, known as *saucisses fumées* and *saucissons fumés*, include *andouille* and the cold-smoked *saucisse de Morteau*. Most meat is smoked using hardwood, but for *saucisse de Morteau* sawdust from conifers such as pine and juniper (common trees in *le jura*, the region's forests) is used.

Boudin noir, the classic pork black pudding, is always fully cooked. Because the 'forcemeat' is liquid before cooking, the sausages are not stuffed but poured into casings, usually using some sort of funnel. Local variations feature other ingredients: versions from Normandy contain apples, while *boudin de Paris* incorporates cooked onions.

Germany

Germans love sausages, and produce over 1,000 varieties. Like the French, they do not distinguish them on a regional basis (with only a few exceptions, for specially favoured types), instead breaking them down into three basic categories. German names for sausages tend to be descriptive, rather than geographic, referring to ingredients, usage or mode of preparation.

The three primary groups are: sausages made entirely from raw ingredients (*Rohwurst*); those containing some pre-cooked ingredients (*Kochwurst*); and those that are cooked after being formed (*Brühwurst*). The basic categories are, in turn, further subdivided.

Rohwurst is fresh, air-cured and fermented, or brined. There are two categories: those that are firm and sliceable, and spreadable ones with high fat content. Smooth-textured *Mettwurst* is all-pork, cured and smoked. *Bauernwurst* ('farmer's sausage', also known as *Knackwurst*, is made from coarsely minced beef and pork, flavoured with marjoram and mustard seeds. *Bratwurst*, known at least since the early fourteenth century, is a cured, smoked, smooth-textured sausage that – in Germany, at least – cannot contain nitrites. Soft, rich *Teewurst* includes bacon, and is smoked over beech wood. *Braunschweiger* is surely the most famous spreadable German liver sausage. *Landjägers* are pocket-sized, air-cured hunter's sausages, pressed to form a rectangular cross section. They are usually served as a pair of links weighing about 225 g (½ lb). Often eaten as snacks, they are occasionally boiled as part of a larger meal.

In *Kochwurst*, pre-cooked meats are often combined with blood or raw organ meats, such as liver. Once encased, it must be refrigerated or frozen. It is further divided into *Blutwurst*, black pudding; *Kochstreichwurst*, meat and liver sausage; and *Sülzwurst*, a sausage bound by gelatine – similar to brawn or the tangy souse, which contains vinegar and/or pickles.

Some, but not all, *Blutwurst* is smoked. Here are just a few variations on the *Blutwurst* theme: *Beutelwurst*, in which the blood is bound with flour, garnished with chunks of fatty bacon, then steamed in a cloth bag; *Grützwurst*, bound with grain (an Austrian variant, *Maischel*, substitutes caul fat for hog casing); *Gutsfleischwurst*, studded with chunks of cooked pork;

and *Zungenwurst*, garnished with pieces of pickled ox-tongue. The name *Thüringer Rotwurst* – the most famous *Blutwurst* – is protected by the European Union.

Kochstreichwurst includes smoked *Leberwurst* from Hesse in central Germany, and a dozen or so similar liver sausages. Hessian *Leberwurst* is not like American liverwurst; its cooked and minced pork is bound with raw liver and stuffed into hog casings before spending time in the smoker. *Kochmettwurst* is a subcategory referring to cooked meat sausages such as *Knack-wurst* and *Pinkels*. *Knackwurst* ('knockwurst' in the USA) is a smoked, garlicky sausage of very finely minced veal and pork. *Pinkels*, or *Pinkelwurst*, is a type of *Grützwurst*, made mostly of bacon and suet, bulked out with barley or oats. It is stuffed into casings and smoked (and occasionally stored in jars, under brine or vinegar).

Sülzwurst is always bound by gelatine, and is usually formed as loaves, while others, such as *Pressack*, are poured into large rounds before cooling. *Schweinkopfsülzwurst* is, as its name

Still-life with Bratwursts and Mustard Pot, oil on canvas, *c.* 1720.

Advertisement, run just before the First World War, featuring gold medals earned in San Francisco, 1894; Turin, 1911; and Chicago, 1893.

suggests, brawn. Other types of *Sülzwurst* may contain ham (*Schinkensülze*), beef tongue (*Zungenwurst*) or blood (*Schwarten-magen rot*).

Brühwurst, 'scalded sausage', is always cooked and must be eaten quickly (unless refrigerated or frozen). It is often a form of *Kochwurst* (sometimes containing cooked horsemeat in the Rhineland), or made with raw ingredients that are only cooked *after* being stuffed in casings. Perhaps the best-known *Brühwurst* is *Weisswurst*, a fresh veal-and-bacon sausage typically seasoned with cardamom, ginger, lemon, mace, onion and parsley. *Weisswurst* is poached and eaten very fresh (usually before noon on the day it is made). It is white because it is unsmoked and contains no nitrites that would turn it pink. Other famous *Brühwurst*s are *Bockwurst*, *Cervelat* and *Jagdwurst*. The relatively modern invention *Bockwurst*, which dates only as far back as 1899, consists of pork and veal, paprika and white pepper. *Cervelat* – descended from the Milanese *cervelado* – is the German (and French and Swiss) equivalent of the hot dog, and just as popular. It is made of beef and pork, with nitrites providing the classic reddish hue. *Jagdwurst* – hunter's sausage – has coarse-textured meat suspended in a smooth, bologna-like matrix, seasoned with cardamom, chillies, garlic, mace and mustard seed.

Zigeunerwurst, 'gypsy sausage', is heavily seasoned with garlic and paprika (another name is *Paprikaspeckwurst*), reflecting tastes the Roma people acquired in their wandering to the southeast of Germany. *Zigeunerwurst* is unusual among traditional German sausages, as Germans generally dislike garlic. They associate its taste (and smell) with gypsies, just as nineteenth-century Americans of British or northern European descent did with Italians and Jews – a piece of culinary bigotry intended to distance swarthy 'lower-class' immigrants from themselves.

Currywurst may be the ultimate in fusion cuisine. German-style sausages travelled to the USA in the nineteenth century, then returned as hot dogs. Legend has it that during the Soviet blockade of Berlin, after the Second World War, an enterprising woman in the British sector combined curry powder with tomato sauce to form a new kind of ketchup, and served it on grilled hot dogs accompanied by French fries. Her invention has become *the* standard street food in Germany – so much so that there is even a museum devoted to it, the Deutsches Currywurst Museum in Berlin.

Great Britain and Ireland

Unlike the Italian climate, Britain's cool, damp weather is not ideal for the production of dry sausages. Consequently, British sausages tend to be cooked, not cured, and used fresh.

British 'puddings' are the basis for all English sausages today. Setting aside the sweet dishes also known as 'desserts', there is a broad range of savoury puddings, from bloodings (a black pudding) to haggis, all the way down to the lowly but much-loved banger. Bangers earned their nickname during the First World War, when water was added to extend the scarce supplies of meat available for making sausage, causing them to burst as they cooked.

Haggis has long been regarded as the quintessential Scottish food – certainly since Robert Burns's poem of 1786 addressing the 'great chieftain o' the pudding-race'. However, it had been popular throughout England long before, and the Highlands may merely be the place to which its popularity retreated (much like mince pies, a medieval dish once eaten year-round, but now served only at Christmas). In fact, the first time haggis was associated with Scotland was in Hannah Glasse's book *The Art of Cookery Made Plain and Easy* (1747). Early English recipes appear in Gervase Markham's *The English Hus-wife* (1615) and Robert May's *The Accomplisht Cook* (1660). Haggis was also known as haggister, and there were sweet versions, such as hackin, which contained beef, dried fruit, oats and sugar. British plum puddings, steamed in cloth rather than a hog's stomach, are descended directly from hackins.[1]

Carle Vernet,
The Sausage Seller,
1816–36, etching.

A saveloy is a fine-textured red sausage, similar to the
frankfurter. The name is derived from French-Swiss *cervelat*,
which in turn goes back to a kind of sausage made from pig's
brains in Renaissance Italy (*cervello* is Italian for 'brain'). In the
nineteenth century, street vendors sold saveloys from big pots
filled with hot water – essentially the same as American hot
dog carts today.

In Wales, faggots resemble baked meatballs made of
bacon, pork mince and offal, wrapped in caul fat. The Welsh
are better known for their Glamorgan sausage, a rare vegetarian sausage containing leeks, breadcrumbs and cheese –
today Caerphilly, because Glamorgan cheese, if available at all,
is hard to find.

Puddings, both black and white, plus small breakfast sausages (as well as bacon) are essential parts of the typical cholesterol-laden breakfast in Ireland. White puddings do not contain blood, and their forcemeat is bulked out with oats (they are eaten all over Britain, as well as in Newfoundland and Nova Scotia). A spicier version, hog's pudding, comes from Cornwall and Devon.

A typical Scottish breakfast includes black pudding and Lorne sausage – square patties of nutmeg- and coriander-seasoned beef and pork, bound with breadcrumbs. Commonly known as 'square sausage', it is not encased; instead the force-meat is chilled in a loaf tin until firm enough to slice, then fried.

The Netherlands

The Netherlands occupies an interesting place in culinary history. While the country itself is small, its ships travelled all over the world, setting up colonies and establishing a trade network that has almost never been rivalled. Dutch sausages have therefore been influenced by remote tropical locations, and Dutch cooking has in turn influenced the encased-meat gastronomy of those places. Its central location among major sausage-eating neighbours has shaped Dutch cuisine. Popular varieties include beef *runderworst* and *metworst*, while *verse worst* refers to any fresh sausages, free of preservatives or curing agents.

In the seventeenth century, the Dutch imported Danish and German oxen to plough the fields that had been reclaimed from the sea. Meat from those animals – seasoned with spices from Dutch ports in the East Indies: cloves, mace, nutmeg and pepper – became the basis of cold-smoked *Amsterdam ossenworste*.

The Iberian Peninsula

The Spanish adapted *lucanicae* (at least etymologically) from the ancient Roman sausage to suit their taste, although they kept to the Roman pattern of black pepper, occasionally perfumed with nutmeg. One version of Spain's *longaniza* features paprika and rosemary. The Portuguese likewise modified Roman *lucanicae* into *linguiça*, adding red chillies after the discovery of the New World.

Spanish versions contain wine, and are cured, dried and smoked. Dark and deeply flavoured, they are often eaten raw – perhaps marinated in olive oil in tapas (the small, salty, appetizer-like dishes most often served with – and intended to increase the consumption of – sherry). They may be cooked by frying or grilling, or sometimes poached in *aguardiente*, a strong grappa-like beverage. Spanish chorizo has many local variants: in texture from fine to coarse; in flavour from *dulce* (mild) to *picante* (hot and spicy) – the differences resulting from the type of paprika used; in degree of dryness and fat content – the harder types eaten raw, while softer, fattier versions (*chorizo fresco*) must be cooked; and in size, most in normal hog casings but others, such as that from Pamplona, that are larger and sliced like salami.

Portuguese *chouriço* has a more intense garlic presence. It is smoked but not dried, so it is cooked before serving. As in Spain, *chouriço* comes in many forms, such as *chouriço de sangue*, a blood sausage; *chouriço de vinho*, made with wine; and *chouriço de ossos*, an unusual sausage containing pieces of bone and cartilage. This last one, understandably, requires long simmering. Similar sausages made by the Basques are called *txorizos*, while in Catalonia they are known as *xoriços*.

Central Europe and the Balkans

We have already seen something of Greek sausages, but have not yet addressed the great traditions of Hungary and Poland. *Kolbász* simply means 'sausage' in Magyar, the language of Hungary. General types include *hurka*, boiled; *májas*, liver; and *véres*, blood. It goes without saying that the Hungarians love paprika, either hot or sweet, but they are also very fond of allspice, caraway, cayenne, garlic, nutmeg and black or white pepper. Their sausages may combine any or all of these seasonings with beef, lamb and pork (or wild boar). Optional sausage ingredients include egg, milk or cream, mushrooms and bulking agents like breadcrumbs or rice (such as the rice in the creamy-textured *véres*, a crisp-skinned black sausage that is first poached, then fried).

The *kielbasa* of Poland, Ukraine and other Slavic regions takes its name from a word for sausage and appears in many phonetic variations. *Kielbasa* is usually smoked, and can be made of any number of different meats: beef (and veal, and even bison), horse, lamb, turkey and – naturally – pork. Polish *kabanosy* are long, thin dried sausages, seasoned only with pepper (no garlic), and made from the flesh of young male pigs that have been fed potatoes; a *kaban* is such a pig.

Kishke, literally 'intestines', are sausages containing a lot of grains, such as barley or buckwheat. Sausages like these have been made at least since the time of Apicius, whose 'white sausage' was stuffed with eggs, emmer wheat and leeks, seasoned with lovage, and studded with pine nuts and peppercorns. *Kishke* are popular all over Eastern Europe and Russia. Polish versions contain beef blood and buckwheat groats, giving them the dark colour usually seen in smoked sausages. They are fairly well known in urban America because Ashkenazy Jews have made them standard deli fare. Obviously, the Jewish versions use no blood or pork; instead *schmaltz* (rendered chicken fat) or beef fat is combined with matzo meal and stuffed into beef intestines.

Ćevapčići (or *cevaps*, or *tchevapchitchi*) have been made in Albania, Bosnia-Herzegovina, Croatia, Macedonia and Serbia at least since the days of the Ottoman Empire. These sausages are un-encased, like some Arabic sausages. The originals used no pork, of course, although modern versions may consist of any combination of beef, lamb, mutton and/or pork, along with garlic and onions.

In Bulgaria, which was once part of Rome's eastern Empire, *lukanka* is more like a French *saucisse* than its Roman namesake. It is firm, somewhat dry and cured, with a white coating of *Penicillium* mould. Unlike the French sausage, it is made from beef and pork, seasoned with cumin. *Lukanka* is stuffed into beef middles (small intestines), like salami, but pressed flat as it dries. Some regional varieties (those from Karlovo, Panagyurishte and Smyadovo) are protected by patents. Romanian blood sausages, known as *sângerete*, are flavoured with basil and pepper. Transylvania – the land of Vlad Dracul – is part of modern Romania, so even the blood sausage is laced with garlic.

4
Sausages from Everywhere Else

Russia

Moving east from Europe, we first meet the sausages of the former Soviet Union. Russia produces numerous sausages, many of which – not surprisingly – are part of the Eastern European tradition. Indeed, during the Soviet days, such countries as Czechoslovakia, Estonia, Hungary, Lithuania, Poland and Ukraine were within what Westerners used to call 'Russia'. Sausages typical of the Soviet satellite countries are still big sellers in today's smaller Russia. In fact, any shop that specializes in sausage is called a *kálbasy*. At first glance, it may seem odd that Russians would love something as 'American' as the hot dog, but frankfurters and their kin are popular street food everywhere else too – so they do.

Officially, Russians have only two types of encased meat – dry and semi-dry – each further divided by quality: higher class, class 1 and class 2 (mutton is used mostly in class 1 and 2 sausages). Perhaps because of the irony of 'classes' of food in a supposedly classless society, in practice there are four categories: cooked, lightly smoked, smoked and 'other' (a catch-all covering blood sausages, liver sausages and brawn).

A possible fifth category, 'Soviet sausages', is a term used more to reflect nostalgia for the time before the break-up of the USSR. Ironically, the sausages made back then were often adulterated with inedible materials, such as lignin, a wood product. Many Russians actually preferred *spoiled* food, because that implied that it had originally been *actual* food.

The United States and the New World

In the interest of world peace – or, at least, *détente* – let's move directly from Russia to America. The New World's populations are composed entirely of immigrants (even the 'indigenous' peoples migrated from Asia, albeit a very long time ago). Immigration always leads to cultural and culinary changes, and often a better selection of sausages.

Little is known about sausages from the pre-colonial period, although it is hard to imagine that Native Americans had not discovered uses for the offal that became sausages elsewhere. Perhaps they never developed a sausage cuisine because they already had a tradition of drying and smoking meats as a means of preservation.

Post-colonial Native Americans (such as the Apaches and Navajos, in the southwest) made blood sausages, and today's Kahnawake Mohawks (originally of northern New York and southern Quebec, but now only near Montreal) still make them. The French and Spanish introduced pigs to the New World in the sixteenth century. It is possible that Native Americans first met blood sausages (*boudin noir* and *morcilla*) that were brought by those early French and Spanish colonists, respectively.

The Cherokee chief Oconastota (whose name means 'Groundhog Sausage') twice visited England – once, in 1762, to meet George III. I have not been able to learn if he was named for sausages that were actually made from the fatty rodents, or if the name referred to 'ground hog', which could of course describe most kinds of sausage. We are on more solid ground in speaking about European immigrants to the New World.

The Van Cortlandt family, who arrived in New York's Hudson Valley in 1639, ordered a copy of the 1683 edition of *The Pleasurable Country Life* from Holland. Originally published in 1667, this virtual encyclopaedia of how to live the good life contained the most popular Dutch cookbook of the time, *The Sensible Cook*. It was the first cookbook in the New World, and it contained two recipes for sausage:

To Make Pig's Sausages
Take three *pond* of chopped meat, two Nutmegs, a *loot* Pepper not too finely crushed, a handful of salt. Knead this together well, fill the intestines not too stiffly; if you want to hang these in the smoke you have to take thicker intestines and place for 2 or 3 days in the brine. One can use half the amount of mutton.

To Make Beef-sausages
In this same manner one makes also Beef-sausages; but one adds also some dried Sage (rubbed fine) but not in those one wants to hang in the smoke, but those must be spiced with Pepper and stuffed into very thick intestines, covered with grey paper, and hung at the side of the chimney.[1]

The cookbook also contained two recipes for grain-based puddings, enriched with lard or beef suet, and one pork-liver sausage seasoned with cloves, mace, nutmeg and pepper. Only the sage could be grown in New Amsterdam; all the other spices came via the Dutch East India Company.

The first English-language cookbook published in the USA was a reprint of Hannah Glasse's *The Art of Cookery Made Plain and Easy* (1747), and chapter 12 was devoted to 'Hogs-puddings, Sausages, &c'. It begins with three 'hog's puddings', flavoured with almonds, sweet spices and either rose water or orange flower water. They are followed by blood pudding and an aside about a Scottish version made with goose blood, stuffed into the goose's neck and baked in a pie filled with goose giblets. Next, Glasse listed two sage-flavoured sausages that are not unlike today's breakfast sausages (one includes a little lemon zest, a variation worth revisiting). The chapter concludes with a recipe for 'Bologna sausages', which looks very similar to what is found in delicatessens today, but for the unspecified 'sweet herbs'.

The first cookbook written in the new country was that by Amelia Simmons, 'an American orphan'. *American Cookery* was published in 1796 with an absurdly long subtitle ending in 'adapted to this country, and all grades of life'. It contained no sausage recipes. While it had many pages of 'puddings', they are all desserts. The first American cookbook to include sausages was Mary Randolph's *The Virginia Housewife; or, Methodical Cook* (1824), and it had but three recipes. One with sage (much like Glasse's) included this advice: 'Sausages are excellent made into cakes and fried, but will not keep so well as in skins.' There was also a black pudding and bologna. Apparently, a taste for the smooth texture of bologna (and later hot dogs) has been part of the American palate from its earliest days.

Lydia Maria Child's *The American Frugal Housewife: Dedicated to Those Who Are Not Ashamed of Economy* (1829) is particularly frugal when it comes to our subject, allotting just 26 words to it: 'Three tea-spoons of powdered sage, one and a half of salt,

Sausages grilling in Arkansas.

and one of pepper, to a pound of meat, is good seasoning for sausages.' Child spends more time on salting and pickling, which were the main ways of preserving meat in America until the advent of refrigeration some decades later.

To understand the place of sausages in American cuisine, we must look beyond the early English and Dutch settlers to the later immigrants. Those immigrants made the country not simply a 'melting pot', but a 'well-seasoned skillet'. When the Acadian French migrated from Nova Scotia to Louisiana, they became known as 'Cajuns'. Cajun *boudins* may have French ancestors, but they have changed a lot since then. French versions often contain milk, while those from Louisiana contain rice. This gives a coarser texture, but also encourages the liberal use of spices, especially cayenne pepper.

The 'Pennsylvania Dutch' are not Dutch; they are immigrants from the Palatine region of Germany, and their cooking is heavily influenced by their European heritage. One sausage-like food especially demonstrates both the connection and the way old recipes adapt to new conditions and ingredients. German *Saumagen*, a stuffed pig's stomach, is known in the u.s. as *hogmal* (pig's maw) or *seimaage*, and is usually baked, not boiled as in Germany. The Pennsylvania Dutch name for it is *g'fillte seimawe*, but non-German Americans sometimes call it Dutch goose. This mildly xenophobic term is roughly analogous to Welsh rabbit or Scotch woodcock, as it brands the 'other' as too cheap or poor to cook 'real' goose, rabbit or woodcock. French goose, similarly, contains no goose (being rather a one-pot dish of sausage, potatoes and vegetables). Lebanon bologna has nothing to do with the Middle East or *mortadella*; it takes its name from Lebanon County, in Pennsylvania Dutch country. This 'sweet bologna' is actually a large, coarse, salami-like summer sausage, made with beef, sugar and sweet spices – cinnamon, cloves and nutmeg. Pennsylvania Dutch rope sausage, a long, unlinked fresh sausage, only looks like coiled rope.

In America's Great Lakes region, from Cleveland to Chicago, coarse-ground summer sausage is known as *praski*

'Bratwurst making at the 100-year-old meat shop', *c.* 1960.

or *prasky*, and is the soft salami typical of sausages made by Central Europeans who settled in the area in the late nineteenth and early twentieth centuries. They came to work in the meat-packing plants and steel mills that were booming owing to centralized shipping via railways and the lakes, and brought with them their taste for sausage.

Today's Americans are squeamish about anything made of blood, but it has not always been that way. There are still communities (beyond Cajun Louisiana) where these 'ethnic' tastes survive. I have eaten Hungarian blood sausage on Manhattan's Upper East Side. Near the Great Lakes, descendants of immigrants keep the blood-sausage tradition alive, while in San Francisco, Italian-Americans make *biroldo* (black pudding laced with pine nuts and raisins).

While American sausages have a European heritage, they became Americanized after arriving on the continent. Bock-wurst, in the USA, is closer to German *Weisswurst*. American bratwursts – the darlings of tailgate parties and backyard barbecues – are nitrite-cured (unlike German *Bratwurst*), and have a reddish colouration not seen in Germany. Texas hot guts are spicier versions of sausages brought by German and Czech immigrants who settled there from the 1830s.

In northern Michigan, everyone knows a sweet, fresh Italian sausage made from pork with cinnamon and cloves, which they call *cudighi*. The word is not Italian, however. It might be a corruption of *cotechino*, but the connection has long passed out of memory. Neither is pepperoni, the most popular topping for pizza in the USA, Italian at all. It is a purely American invention that is related to spicy salame from Calabria (*soppressata*) and Naples (*salsiccia Napoletana piccante*).

Bologna, or 'baloney', resembles its ancestral *mortadella* in its fine-textured emulsion and colour (essentially the same forcemeat used in American hot dogs). This child-friendly cold cut is called 'jumbo' in the area around Pittsburgh, Pennsylvania. While *mortadella* is garnished with cubes of fat, American delicatessens sell 'olive loaf', a rectangular slab of bologna studded with pimento-stuffed olives.

Salami, almost always eaten thinly sliced on sandwiches, has found its way into American culture through various ethnic routes. Traditional versions, like those found in France and Italy – complete with white *Penicillium* mould – were first made in San Francisco. Italian-American sausage-makers fought a long battle with the U.S. Department of Agriculture to allow the slowly air-cured sausages to be manufactured there, in a climate whose conditions closely matched those of Europe's great salame regions. Much more common are the hard salami and Genoa salami seen in delicatessens, generic sliced cold cuts in synthetic casings. Kosher salamis, made from beef and (today) stuffed into cellulose casings, were first made in New York City's Lower East Side. Katz's, the last great New York deli, still uses the slogan it created during the Second World War: 'Send a salami to your boy in the army.'

Portuguese immigrants settled in coastal U.S. towns, especially in New England. Rhode Islanders consume large quantities of *chouriço* and *linguiça* on sandwiches and pizza (it is one of the few places in America where pepperoni is *not* the pizza topping of choice). There are also pockets of Portuguese immigrants in Hawaii. The Hawaiian version, called simply Portuguese sausage, is softer than its predecessor, and has acquired a sweet island flavour that the Portuguese (or Romans) would never expect, but which seems perfectly natural in the Islands.

One would think that Canadian breakfast sausage would resemble something from their French-English heritage. Not so. Linkies are small hot dog-like sausages, larger than a Vienna sausage, but just as pink. Canadians do make a range of

British-style sausages, but not for breakfast. They have adopted other Old World sausages (and adapted them, occasionally modifying them to incorporate Canadian ingredients, such as game and maple syrup). Their take on *kielbasa* is *kubasa*, or kubie (when eaten in a bun as a hot dog).

Boudin noir migrated with French colonists to the Antilles where, as in Louisiana, the subtle Gallic sausage was transformed to meet local taste and ingredients (*boudin antillais* incorporates indigenous allspice and fiery Scotch bonnet chillies). Scotch bonnets also ignite black sausages in Trinidad and Tobago.

Latin Americans – who today still speak the language of sixteenth-century conquistadores – have adopted and adapted many sausage styles and names from the Old World. Of course, as they travelled to the New World, their recipes mutated into a host of different sausages, often sharing etymological links with their ancient Roman past. The *longaniza* of Argentina and Uruguay are fermented until dry, which lends them a tangy sweetness that is heightened by aniseed. Mexican *longaniza*, like their chorizo (but unlike *its* Spanish ancestor), is pungent with hot chillies. In Puerto Rico, the sausage looks as red as the Mexican version, but the colour comes from annatto seed (*Bixa orellana*). Cuban, Dominican and Puerto Rican *longaniza* are stuffed into long lengths of hog casing and air-dried. While most *longaniza* starts with pork, Puerto Ricans sometimes add – or substitute – poultry, such as chicken or turkey.

The smoked paprika of Spain and Portugal is not used in the chorizos of the Americas. Instead, hot red chillies – without smoke – season most Latin American chorizos. Curiously, the closer Spanish-speaking countries are to the mother country, the more similar their tastes; Cuban, Dominican and Puerto Rican chorizos are less hot, and smokier, than those from regions to the west and south.

Green chorizo sausage, Toluca, Mexico.

Mexican chorizo is typically made of pork, but can also contain beef or venison. It is fermented to develop its lactic acid tanginess (although it may also contain a little vinegar, in place of the white wine used in the Spanish version). Occasionally it is dried, but most often it is used fresh, like Spanish *chorizo fresco*. It may be stuffed into hog casings, although commercially made chorizo is often sold in synthetic casings, or sold unstuffed, since it is generally cooked in crumbled form. *Chorizo de bolita* is stuffed into hog casings, but tied into short, spherical links (*bolita* means 'little pellet' or 'bullet'). Most Mexican chorizo is red; the carotenoid pigments in chillies are oil-soluble, so their rendered fat is a deep red-orange.

Spanish and Portuguese *embutidos* and Catalan *embotits* – generic terms for sausage – have found their way into Latin American cuisine as well. Typically, *embutidos* are flavoured with herbs and spices that vary in different regions, but are likely to consist of chillies, cloves, garlic, ginger, nutmeg, paprika, rosemary and/or thyme.

Mexican chorizos are used fresh, often without their casings. They are spicier than Spanish chorizos, with a decided tang – either from lactic-acid fermentation or added vinegar. In south-central Mexico, some unusual Tolucan *embutidos* feature coriander and tomatillos (or spinach and pine nuts), and so are called *chorizos verdes*. *Chorizo verde de Toluca* (green chorizo of Toluca) is made with coriander, roasted jalapeño chillies and vegetables and herbs, such as chard, spinach, parsley and tomatillos. In Mexico, *chorizo verde* can be purchased in two forms: a frighteningly garish one prepared with green food colouring, or a more drab one that gets its colour only from the vegetables listed above. Charcuterie is so pervasive in Toluca that its citizens use 'chorizo' as a nickname for virtually anything (a tool, a rock, a person, *anything*). In addition to chorizos

Butifarra, from a Colombian street vendor.

of various colours, Tolucans make *longanizas* and *obispos* (a local blood sausage).

Further down the Central American isthmus, the *chorizo Salvadoreño* of El Salvador is a mixture of beef, pork fat and bacon, seasoned with black pepper, cumin, garlic, onion, oregano, thyme and vinegar. It contains no paprika and only a little chilli; it gets its reddish colour from ground seeds of *achiote* (annatto). It is always eaten fresh. Ecuadorian chorizo, like the Salvadorian version, glows with *achiote*, but is flavoured with cinnamon and garnished with whole peppercorns.

'Chorizo' is a generic name for any coarsely ground sausage in Argentina (where it is mildly seasoned and composed mostly of beef), and also in Colombia and Uruguay. The term *chorizo español* refers, in those countries, specifically to the kind of sausage found in the old country.

Brazilian *chouriço* does not resemble Spanish, Portuguese or Latin American chorizo. Instead, the name refers to a blood sausage, more like *morcilla*. What Brazil's neighbours call chorizo, Brazilians call *linguiça*.

Africa, the Middle East and Australasia

Africa has less of a sausage tradition than many places, possibly because of its climate. However, in a few countries – especially those that were colonized extensively by cultures that *do* enjoy encased meats – some regional sausages have emerged.

Merguez is found all over North Africa (and in France, owing to immigration from Algeria, Morocco and Tunisia). *Saucisse merguez d'agneau* is made with lamb, while *saucisse merguez de boeuf* is beef and *saucisse merguez d'agneau et boeuf*, obviously, contains both. The Egyptian sausage *mombar mahshy* combines beef, lamb and rice, seasoned with cardamom and mastic (a resinous gum that smells like cedar, from the shrub *Pistacia lentiscus*).

Coarse-textured *boerewors* is a traditional pork sausage in South Africa that may also contain beef fat, mutton or veal, seasoned with cloves, coriander, nutmeg and pepper. *Wors* is Dutch for 'sausage', and a *boer* is a farmer, descended from the original Dutch settlers in the region. This is a local take on Dutch *verse worst*, in one continuous unlinked spiral. South African *boerewors* variations include *garlic wors*, *kameeldoring*, *karoowors* and *spekwors*. *Droëwors* is a fine-textured Afrikaner version of Dutch *metworst*. The British influence can be seen in the popularity of red puddings, although, oddly enough, the South African slang term for these Scottish sausages is 'Russians'.

Islamic and Jewish dietary restrictions make pork (and/or blood) sausages rare in the Middle East, but lamb or beef *merguez* and *makanek* are popular (in Lebanon, they are sometimes glazed with pomegranate molasses). Some sausages are made from poultry (chicken or goose) in compliance with the Muslim and Jewish rules of *shariah* and *kashrut* respectively. In Iran, for example, one can find salami and bologna made from chicken, or beef '*mortodella*'; one company sells a variety of sausages made from beef, veal, chicken, turkey and ostrich. Hard-dried *sujuk* is made from beef in the Islamic Middle East and Central Asia, pork in the Christian parts of the Balkans, and horseflesh in Kazakhstan and Kyrgyzstan. Regional spices include cumin, garlic, hot chillies and sour sumac. The sausage meat is sometimes made as *shawarma*, a spicy Turkish variation on Greek *gyros* (large spit-roasted forcemeat that is shaved off for service, exposing the underlying meat to the flames). Kasakhstan's *kazy* are dried, smoked sausages, filled with salted horseflesh and garlic.

In Lebanon, *makanek* (or *maqaniq*) comes in two versions, according to the religion of the sausage-maker (and -eater). Muslim versions are made with beef and lamb, stuffed into narrow sheep casings. Christian versions contain pork, cognac and white wine. Both are heavily spiced with cloves, coriander, cumin, nutmeg, pepper and vinegar, garnished with toasted pine nuts and juicy with fat – up to 50 per cent by weight.

In India, in addition to the restrictions on pork (for Muslims), beef is proscribed for Hindus, so chicken, mutton and turkey sausages are popular. One brand, 'Mr Singh's Bangras', puns on British 'bangers', but has flavours reminis-cent of the Middle East: dried fruits such as apricots and dates, along with sweet and pungent spices, including cardamom, cloves and ginger, and orange zest. Jains and most Buddhists (especially those following precepts of the Mahayana sutras) are vegetarian, although Buddhists have a word for sausage: *maṃsavaṭṭikāvisesa*.

In Tibet, where a vegetarian diet would be difficult to maintain (since very little grows there), Buddhists consume several kinds of meat and dairy foods. In fact, they make *gyurma* sausages of sheep or yak blood with toasted barley meal, flavoured with *emma* (Tibetan for Sichuan pepper, *Zanthoxylum piperitum*; a similar sausage, without blood, is called *gyucar*); a boiled sausage of dog meat; another of mutton and sheep fat; one made with liver; a deep-fried one made from sheep's lungs; and a nearly vegetarian one of flour (or meal) and oil.

'Snag' is Australian for 'British-style sausage' (Aussies are masters of colourful slang). German immigrants settled parts of southern Australia, and *Mettwurst* is still popular there – not imported from the old country, but produced by a number of Australian companies. German sausage, a *mortadella*-like luncheon meat, has borne a British-sounding name (Devon) since the First World War, when patriotic fervour forced the renaming of a sausage that had never been German anyway. Curiously, veal German is just Devon with a small amount of red wine flavouring added – but *its* name never changed. Saveloys also experienced de-Germanization: before the war they were known as frankfurters. New Zealanders shorten the name to savs, unless the sausages themselves are shortened to the size of Vienna sausages, in which case they are called cheerios. Cabanossi – which sounds like an Italian sausage – is more like a slender, lightly smoked *kielbasa* stuffed into sheep casings. It is neither as dry nor as heavily smoked as Polish *kabanosy*.

Asia

The Chinese have made sausages since about 600 BC. They originally used goat meat or lamb – despite the fact that they were the first people to domesticate wild pigs, in about 4000 BC. Pork is one of the best-loved foods in China (there is a very funny essay by Charles Lamb, 'A Dissertation upon Roast Pig', about the accidental discovery of roast pork by a Chinese farmer), so it is surprising that pork was not the first choice as a sausage ingredient.

Lop cheung (*kun chiang*, *yuen chang*) – sweet, dry sausages typically flavoured with garlic and pepper – may include typical Chinese ingredients (ginger, rice wine, soy sauce). They are unsmoked, and are used only in cooked dishes. *Mi xue gao* and *xue chang* are blood sausages, while *bairouxue chang* contains some pork as well. *Ren chang* is made from duck livers.

Chinese sausages show considerable regional variation. Those from Sichuan are hotter, and reddened by chilli powder (they also contain Sichuan peppercorns, giving them a curious numbing quality). Taiwanese *xiang chang* ('fragrant sausage') is sweeter than *lop cheung*. In Manchuria, *hong chang* – a smoked sausage resembling *kielbasa* – was introduced by a German sausage-maker during the Japanese occupation in the 1930s.

Sausages made of spleen, liver and other organ meats are common throughout Southeast Asia. They are heavily laced with garlic, supposedly to protect perishable meats during the drying period in the hot and humid climate.

In Thailand, Vietnam's fish-sauced pork *giò lụa* is called *moo yor*. *Kai yor* is similar, substituting chicken for pork. *Chiang Mai*, a Thai sausage with a Chinese name, uses distinctive Thai ingredients: chillies, coriander leaves and stems, fish sauce (*nam pla*), galangal, kaffir lime leaves and lemongrass.

Thai sour sausages – *naem muu* and the northeastern *sai krok Isan* (Isaan sausage) – are fermented, although cheap imitations, overloaded with rice and garlic, substitute citric acid (and taste, unsettlingly, like artificial lime). Both genuine and adulterated versions are familiar street foods. Occasionally appearing as 'herb sausage', *sai krok Isan* may be flavoured with

A display of Chinese sausage at Changi Airport, Singapore.

Sai krok Isan, grilled fermented pork and sticky rice Thai sausage.

lemongrass or the leaves of bergamot oranges, *nam pla* and/or the ubiquitous pastes of chillies and shrimp.

Naem begins with raw pork and strips of cooked pigskin, along with garlic and hot chillies. It is traditionally wrapped in banana leaves (although synthetic casings are now common), and left to ferment in Thailand's heat for three days. The result, sour and pungent, is quintessentially Thai. A similar sour sausage made by the Hmong people is formed in short, almost-round links, then fried as an appetizer. *Sai krok lueat* are curry-flavoured Thai blood sausages (with cellophane noodles standing in for the usual rice or grains), while the Vietnamese versions (*dôi tiêt* or *dôi huyêt*, from the north and south respectively) show their fondness for basil, coriander and shrimp paste. The Vietnamese also like Chinese sausage, which they call *lap xuong*. Burmese sausages are made either of pork (*wet u gyaung*) or of chicken (*kyet u gyaung*).

Sundae (or *soondae*), Korean sausages, are often made with blood or seafood, such as squid (*ojing eo sundae*) or pollack

Street sausage vendor in Chiang Mai, Thailand.

(*myeongtae sundae*), and generally boiled or steamed. Like Thai blood sausages, Korean *sundae* are filled with cellophane noodles, but the resemblance ends there. Koreans love *doenjang* (a miso-like soybean paste), perilla leaves (a type of mint) and spring onions – so all these are tossed into the sausage machine. The meat is usually padded out with bean sprouts, sticky rice and the omnipresent fermented vegetables collectively known as *kimchi*. *Sundae* are for Koreans what hot dogs are for Americans – street food – although some restaurants specialize in them.

The Japanese have no sausage-making tradition. In fact, it is possible that they did not begin producing sausages before the First World War. At that time, German prisoners of war being held in a Japanese internment camp in Narashino, just east of Tokyo, were ordered to demonstrate the methods used in the production of a dozen varieties of sausage. Yoshifusa Iida, an official who was interested in

Vietnamese sausages (*doi*) typically served with a pile of fresh herbs.

meat-processing methods, disseminated what he learned from the POWs. Those early attempts to adapt the methods to Japanese taste were not successful. In 1934, hot dogs were sold at an exhibition baseball game in the city of Nishinomiya, with Babe Ruth playing for the American team. The unfamiliar food was not a hit (many spectators ate only the rolls, throwing out the sausage). However, after the Second World War, the need for more processed foods led to the development of pork- and seafood-based sausages. By 1952, mass-produced fish sausages, made from Alaskan haddock, went to market. Today, 'fish' sausage is also made from salmon and whale. *Paripori* pork sausage supposedly takes its name, onomatopoetically, from the characteristic 'snap' made when one bites into a juicy sausage with a natural casing.

In the Philippines, both Spanish and Chinese influences are evident; any dried sausage is called 'chorizo' – even Chinese *lop cheung*. Chorizo Bilbao, however, more closely resembles the Spanish sausage. Philippine *longganisa* may be based on beef, chicken or tuna, and comes in a wide range of local variations, from the salty *longaniza* of Guagua, through the Lucban, Tuguegarao and Vigan garlic-infused sausages, to the *longganisang hamonado* of Baguio, sweetened with fruit juice.

The Spanish and Portuguese did not form colonies only in the Americas. The colony in Goa, on the Indian coast, was under Portuguese rule for almost half a millennium – and still has a very spicy variant of *chouriço*, albeit one that is influenced by South Asian taste. It adds cumin, ginger and turmeric to the usual Portuguese spice mixture. Goan *chouriço* can be 'wet', 'dry' or 'skin'. 'Wet' is cured for about a month, while 'dry' spends at least a season in the sun. 'Skin' gets its name from one of its primary ingredients, lots of chewy pigskin. Goan *chouriços* can be had in hot or mild versions, in sizes large or small.

In Goa, 'sausages' refers to something very similar to *longaniza*, although their heat comes not from chillies but from black pepper. To add confusion, they are commonly known as Goan frankfurters, despite not at all resembling hot dogs.

5
Technology and the Modern Sausage

So far, we have seen hints about some of the technical problems inherent in the production of sausage, and they will be addressed in more detail here. Parts of this are scientific or historical, while others help home sausage-makers to produce safer, more desirable sausages on their own. Serious amateurs and/or budding professionals should consult some of the books and websites listed in the bibliography.

Seasonality

Before the end of the nineteenth century, sausages were made primarily in the winter months, because meat spoiled quickly during the rest of the year, and feeding pigs was expensive when they could not forage for themselves. When artificial refrigeration became available, and railways facilitated the cheap transport of live animals and feed to large processing plants in urban centres like Chicago, year-round production became possible and profitable.

Making link sausages, Swift & Co.'s Packing House, Chicago, *c.* 1905.

Preparing the Forcemeat

Originally, all forcemeats were chopped by hand, with knives or by rocking a special curved blade – known as a *mezzaluna* – that matched the inner contours of a wooden bowl. Very smooth textures like that of *mortadella* were obtainable only by pounding. (The name *mortadella*, however, comes not from the big mortars and pestles once used in the sausage's production,

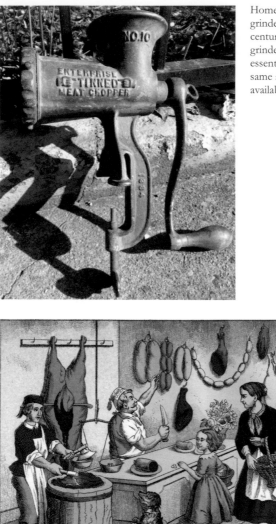

Home meat grinder, 19th century. This grinder is essentially the same as models available today.

An illustration from a German children's book of the 1880s. Note the two-handed method used for chopping the meat.

Edward L. Loper, *Sausage Grinder*, c. 1937.

but from the myrtle berries used to flavour it.) Sometimes, the mortar was just a hollowed-out tree stump.

By the 1880s commercial meat grinders had begun to replace knives as the preferred method for 'chopping' meat. Some used complex sets of revolving blades that mimicked the way a butcher would chop meat. Others, more like home meat mincers, used a 'worm' to feed meat past a rotating blade shaped like a propeller. Each of its four blades slid across a die drilled with holes of a specific size. In effect, each blade and hole acted like a tiny pair of scissors, cutting the meat into pieces of the desired diameter. According to the food historian Anne Mendelson,

> The worm-feed machines with rotary handles were a great stimulus to sausage-making. I would bet that most of the

The German equivalent to the U.S. Buffalo Chopper, both high-speed cutters that don't cause heat-producing friction.

Advertisement for home sausage grinders, in Colonel Arthur Kenney-Herbert's *Fifty Breakfasts: A Splendid Victorian Collection of Over 130 Classic Breakfast Recipes* (1894).

sausages being commercially sold in Europe and America at the turn of the twentieth century came into being only after the advent of mechanical grinders.[1]

Grinders made the production of sausages much less labour-intensive, and the advent of electric motors a few decades later, made the mass production of sausages possible.

While most sausages today contain mechanically minced meats, some artisans still use knife-cut meats. *Salame tradizionale di Fabriano* and *salame storico di Fabriano*, from the Italian region of Marche, contain finely minced lean pork, garnished with large hand-cut chunks of white fat. The pork for *Rivello soperzata* is finely minced, by hand, stuffed into hog casings and pressed.

Salting and Seasoning

Salt, in sausage, serves three functions: it helps to preserve perishable meats, killing some bacteria that could cause spoilage (salt's preservative powers will be addressed later in this chapter); it dissolves a portion of the protein (myosin) in the meats, which, when cooked, forms a smooth binding matrix for the bits of meat in the sausage; and finally, it adds or enhances flavour.

The same process is used by fast-food companies to form scraps of otherwise unsaleable meat (tongue, heart, tripe, skin, and so on) into more appetizing form, such as 'nuggets' or 'filets'. Much of such meat is recovered from bones, industrially, and would be unrecognizable – and unsaleable – without the transformative binding powers of salt. This mechanically recovered meat, called 'pink slime', has been the subject of widespread media attention reminiscent of the furore that followed the publication of Upton Sinclair's book *The Jungle* in 1906.

The sausage-maker (or processor) can easily see when soluble proteins have been released by the salt: the minced meat mixture becomes sticky. The ratio of ingredients necessary for this binding to occur is simple: 13 g of salt per kilogram of meat (or 1 oz for every 5 lb). (Salt is not the only ingredient that has been used to bind together the bits of protein and seasonings in sausages; the others will be addressed in the next chapter.) Salt also reinforces the flavours of other seasonings. This is especially important in sausages that are served cold, since volatile flavour compounds are not released as freely in cold as in hot foods.

Traditionally, herbs and spices are added to the force-meat, either before or after grinding, depending on the desired appearance of the finished sausage. In some sausages, whole spices (such as peppercorns or fennel seeds) function as garnishes, providing a tiny burst of contrasting flavour when they are bitten into. Many mass-produced sausages – such as hot dogs – no longer contain actual herbs and spices, but substitute extracts or oleoresins for the original seasonings. This produces a more uniform product (eliminating variability in the raw ingredients), more even mixing and a smooth consistency. It is also cheaper.

Stuffing and Packaging

Sausages can be stuffed using something as simple as a funnel, a tapered horn that attaches to a home meat mincer (hand-cranked or electric) or various kinds of piston devices. Industrially, gigantic computer-controlled machines fill, form and package thousands of sausages per minute.

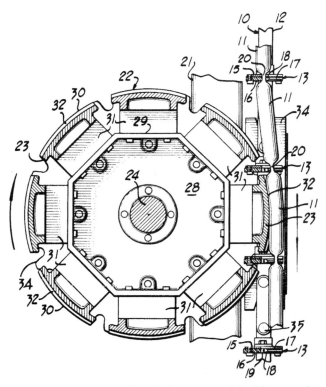

Illustration of a mechanism for releasing connected frankfurters as they come out of the processing chambers. Designed by R. J. Millenaar and E. G. Blair for Oscar Meyer & Company.

Sausage-makers have their own terminology for the various intestines used as casings. They are distinguished by anatomy, and sometimes species. Natural casings include 'bungs' or caecums (the closed bulges found at the top end of the large intestine), the largest natural casings (hog bungs are filled with liverwurst or chunks of ham, in *culatello*); 'middles', large intestines, typically used for salami; 'rounds' or small intestines, the most common size of casing, including those from sheep (breakfast links, chipolatas) and hogs (Italian sausage, bratwurst). Animals of different ages provide a wide range of sausage sizes. Bovine casings (useful for large sausages, or when pork is proscribed) include ox runners, small intestines used for large salamis, and ox middles, sometimes mistakenly called haggis bungs, which provide the large diameter needed for *mortadella*.

Modern technology provides a number of alternatives. Some, for the convenience of the producers, provide uniform, safe and machine-friendly alternatives to the variability of natural casings. Some are compatible with Jewish *kashrut* and Islamic *shariah* laws. Synthetic casings, made of cellulose, collagen or plastic, are available in many sizes and colours. They are often used for spreadable pâté-like preparations (such as *Braunschweiger*), salamis (especially kosher beef salamis) and other commercial cold meats (such as bologna).

Some sausages do not seem like 'encased meats' – because they aren't. Today's skinless franks, for example, are not actually skinless. Their emulsion of finely minced meat and seasonings is practically a liquid before it is cooked (the commercial

Standard hog casings – on the right, packed in salt; on the left, soaked in warm water and ready for stuffing.

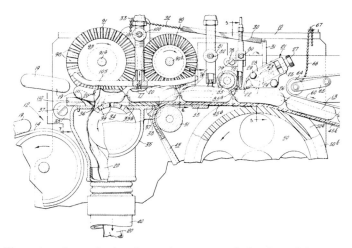

Illustration of a mechanism for continuous removal of casings of tiny 'skinless' frankfurters. Designed by W. A. von Lersner and E. F. Brown for the Campbell Soup Company.

term is 'batter'). It flows into cellulose casings on a continuous machine that fills and cooks the hot dogs, then slits and peels off the casing before packaging them.

Curing

Sausages are cured – protected from spoilage – through drying and the action of various organisms that convert sugars in the meat to lactic acid, effectively lowering the pH (increasing acidity) to a level that is inhospitable to harmful bacteria.

Bacteria can be controlled by chemical means, either naturally or artificially. Salt acts as a preservative in two ways: it helps to draw moisture from the meat, effectively lowering it below the level at which pathogens can thrive; and it increases the osmotic pressure within the cells of bacteria, causing them to burst.

Nitrites and nitrates have long been used to inhibit the growth of dangerous bacteria, such as *Clostridium botulinum*, the organism that causes botulism. *Botellus* (an ancient Roman type of sausage, which in turn got its name from the word for intestine) gives us the English word for botulism, though sausages were not responsible for the disease. Émile van Ermengem identified the bacteria in Belgium in 1823 while investigating several cases of the disease caused by badly preserved ham. Looking through a microscope, he noticed that the bacteria looked like tangled strings of sausage links, hence the species name.[2]

Other undesirable organisms in sausage production include *Staphylococcus aureus*, several strains of *Salmonella*, certain yeasts and moulds – although *Penicillium* moulds (the white coating on some dried sausages) prevent the growth of harmful bacteria and add flavour.

Before sausages are adequately dried they are subject to spoilage, so a curing salt containing a nitrite (NO_2) compound is used to prevent the development of *C. botulinum*. Sausage-makers commonly incorporate nitrite by adding tinted cure mix (TCM; coloured pink to avoid confusion with ordinary salt). TCM is salt combined with 6.25 per cent sodium nitrite ($NaNO_2$). It is also known as Prague powder or Instacure #1, and is used for meats that are hot-smoked (cooked) and will not be stored for long periods. Instacure #2 adds sodium *nitrate* ($NaNO_3$) as well. It is used for meats that are to be cold-smoked – or not smoked at all – and kept for extended periods.

Both curing mixtures release nitric oxide (NO_2) to oxidize dangerous bacteria. It also combines with haemoglobin and myoglobin to produce a pigment that turns deep pink when heated (creating the characteristic rosy appearance of cooked ham and salami). The nitrate in Instacure #2 continues to release NO_2 after the nitrite has been exhausted, which is why it is preferred for cold-smoked, longer-cured meat products.

Naturally occurring nitrates and nitrites (such as those in celery) have been used to preserve meat for centuries. However, in England in 1956 John Barnes and Peter Magee found that one nitrosamine (formed when proteins plus nitrates were exposed to high heat) could cause tumours in laboratory animals. Later tests showed a high level of correspondence between nitrosamines in animal feed and the development of cancers.[3] These discoveries led to changes in the way these compounds are used commercially. Nitrites, used in reduced quantities (120 parts per million) and in the presence of vitamin C ($C_6H_8O_6$, ascorbic acid) or ERY ($C_6H_7NaO_8$, sodium erythorbate), do not develop the carcinogens once found in overcooked meats containing potassium or sodium nitrates (KNO_3 or $NaNO_3$, saltpetre).

Not all bacteria are harmful, however. *Lactobacilli* convert natural sugars in meat to lactic acid, lowering its pH. The increased acidity discourages harmful bacteria in the same way as nitrite/nitrate mixtures: by oxidizing them. Traditional sausage-makers have used ambient micro-organisms to start fermentation, leading to local variations in flavour, attributed to *terroir*. Modern methods usually involve inoculation with approved strains of *Bifidobacterium*, *Lactobacilli*, *Pediococcus* and *Staphylococcus*, as well as *Lactococcus lactis* (which produces the tang in sauerkraut) and *Streptococcus lactis*. Today, some yeasts (*Debaryomices hansenii* and *Saccharomyces cerevisiae*) produce the desired acid levels. Sometimes the pH is adjusted by adding chemicals, such as sodium acid pyrophosphate (for hot dogs or bologna-like sausages) or glucono delta lactone (for cured sausages, such as Genoa salami).[4] Most cured sausage recipes include sugar, or glucose, to provide added nutrients for the lactic acid-producing bacteria to achieve the desired pH.

Slow fermentation creates deeper, more complex flavours than mere seasoning could produce. Mexican chorizos have a lactic-acid sharpness (although some quickly produced versions simply contain added vinegar – diluted acetic acid – or citric acid, instead of waiting for fermentation to work). Chemical additives provide the desired sourness, but are not as effective as lactic acid in preventing spoilage; such sausages must be refrigerated and used quickly. More intense seasoning makes up for the lack of the complex flavours found in fermented sausages.

Smoking

Smoking acts as a preservative by adding a number of phenolic compounds found in the smoke, and by forming a tough coating on the outside of the sausage. This impervious layer is known as the pellicle, and can form only if the sausage is air-dried briefly before being smoked. Particles in the smoke adhere to the pellicle, producing its characteristic dark colour. Smoke also adds flavour to sausages, and their taste and texture vary according to the temperature at which they are smoked, and the kind of wood used. Most are smoked over hardwoods (such as alder, apple, maple and oak), although in a few exceptions conifers are used. Hot-smoked meats (74–85°C/165–85°F) are fully cooked, and can be eaten as they are; cold-smoked (38°C/100°F) meats must be either cooked or dried to safe moisture-content levels before being consumed. Because the precise levels of smoky flavour and colour are difficult to achieve consistently, many commercial sausages (especially hot dogs) are passed through a cloud of nebulized liquid smoke instead of spending time in a smokehouse.

6
Sausage: Theme and Variations

Blood

Pig's blood is commonly used to make sausages or black puddings, although cow's blood can also serve. Some religious scriptures (Jewish *kashrut* and Islamic *shariah*) forbid the consumption of blood. For both, eating pig's blood is doubly proscribed.

Blood contains no myosin, the protein found in muscle tissue, so salt is not used for binding as in other sausages. Instead it is used for flavour – and is stirred into the fresh blood to prevent it from forming fibrin (clots of insoluble protein) that would yield an unpleasant texture.

Being a liquid, blood is handled differently from other forcemeats. Cooked grains, such as rice, are often added to provide bulk and make it easier to stuff into casings, especially for blood sausages. Because their 'forcemeat' begins as a liquid, blood sausages cannot be grilled or fried directly; they are always poached first. That denatures the protein in the plasma, making it firm enough to slice. Norwegian *blodpølse* and Hungarian *véres* typically contain rice, contributing to their creamy texture. Scottish oatmeal, combined with cow's blood, makes black pudding cakes, while Norwegian *blodpudding* contains rice and barley. Estonian *verivorst* also contains whole barley. In *sfarricciato*, a blood sausage from the Molise region of southern Italy, cooked emmer wheat provides the needed texture.

French *boudin noir de porc* is garnished with lightly fried onions and cubes of fat, seasoned with sweet spices (cloves or allspice, sometimes in the form of *quatre épices*). The Novarese of Piedmont make *marzapane*, which sounds like a sweet, but is definitely savoury; it contains bacon, garlic, milk and wine. The *samurchio* of Naples contains cow's blood flavoured with chilli and bay leaves, while Tuscany's *biroldo di Lucca* combines sweet spices, pine nuts and raisins with cow's blood. Sardinian *su zurette* is similar, substituting ovine blood. Umbria's *sanguinaccio* is perfumed with orange zest.

Basques have their own blood sausage, *morcilla*. It travelled from the Pyrenees to the New World, where in Argentina it is known as *morcilla a la vasca*. If some diners shudder at the thought of consuming blood, the other ingredients of this sausage might cause them to faint in horror: 'cleaned pig's head, kidneys, diaphragm and other organs not to be used elsewhere'.[1] While many blood sausages make use of sweet spices, this one also contains cumin, garlic, oregano and fried spring onions.

German *Kartoffelwurst* is simply *Blutwurst* garnished with diced potato. Scrapple-like Dutch and German *balkenbrij* sometimes contains blood. Perhaps the most unusual blood sausage is made in Tibet: called *gyurma*, it is made from yak blood.

Other Offal

Sheep's lungs fill casings in Turkish *kokoreç*, and Greeks make a kind of *andouillette* from the heart, intestines, kidneys and lungs (plus garlic, oregano, thyme and almonds), baked in olive oil and lemon juice. Greek Jews call the same sausage *gardoumbes*. In the southern Italian region of Campania, lungs provide the protein for *salsiccia di polmone*, while in northern Germany smoked *Lungenwurst* is made from pork and lungs.

German *Milzwurst* is garnished with pieces of spleen, while Tuscan *ammazzafegato* incorporates heart, kidneys, liver, spleen and tongue, along with actual pork flesh. Uzbekistan's pungent *hasip* is filled with minced lamb or beef, along with kidneys, lungs and spleen (and a little rice).

Americans generally do not want to know about offal, let alone eat it – but immigrant preferences sometimes make exceptions to the rule. Charlie Hasselback, a German American from western Pennsylvania, moved to Texas at the end of the nineteenth century. His Pittsburgh hot links – all-beef sausages packed with ground-up hearts, salivary glands, tongues and tripe – are a Texas staple today, and not just in German communities.

Unusual Seasonings

Soft, sweet Sardinian *sa supressada sanguinaccio* is made with pecorino cheese, mint, raisins, sugar, thyme and cooked greens. The *baldonazzio sanguinaccio*, or *brusti*, of Trentino-Alto Adige in northern Italy feature cooked onions and leeks, chestnut flour, walnuts and raisins, seasoned with nutmeg and savory. In the south of the country, an Apulian blood pudding contains citron, chocolate, cinnamon, cloves, pine nuts, sugar and vanilla; while *sfarricciato*, a sweet blood pudding from Molise, contains cocoa, orange peel, sugar, raisins, pine nuts and walnuts.

Like most Italians, Lombards make their own version of the ancient Roman *luganega*. What distinguishes theirs is the

Orecchiette ('little ears'), with sweet Italian sausage and broccoli rabe.

combination of seasonings: cinnamon, cloves, pepper, musk, nutmeg, rose wine, saffron, sugar – garnished with pine nuts and raisins. John Nott's *The Cooks and Confectioners Dictionary* (1723) featured a recipe for an unusual sausage made of beef marrow, eggs, ground almonds, rose water and sugar. *Cotechino cremonese vaniglia* from Cremona is another perfumed sausage, but featuring vanilla.

Not Your Usual Mammals

Goats are one of the most-consumed meat animals on the planet, yet they are frequently forgotten in the so-called First World. Goat meat is substituted for other meats in many of the world's sausages. Lombard *salame di capra* is a dry, cured sausage made with goat, as well as pork, *pancetta*, red wine and garlic. Uzbekistan's *khassip* incorporates goat's lung and kidney and spleen, seasoned with cumin. Dried German *Ziegenknacker* is also made from goat.

Horseflesh is the basis of *kazi*, in Turkic Central Asia (Kazakhstan, Kyrgyzstan and Tatarstan). Salted, garlicky force-meat is stuffed into horse intestines, then smoked or air-dried. Sausages made with horse are also popular in Siberia. The journalist Peter Lund Simmonds reported a few cases in the nineteenth century in which horsemeat was used to adulterate sausages in England and the USA, where its consumption was considered an abomination.[2] In the mid-nineteenth century, a committee investigating the adulteration of British foodstuffs heard this testimony:

> the hindquarters of horses . . . are generally sold to mix
> with collared brawn, or pig's heads, as they are called
> with us, and for sausages and polonies. I understand,
> also, from those in the habit of making them, that horse-
> flesh materially assists the making of sausages; it is a
> hard fibrin, and it mixes better, and keeps them hard, and

Heavily smoked *mahan*, a traditional Turkic sausage made from horse flesh.

they last longer in the shop window before they are sold, because otherwise the sausages run to water, and become soft and pulpy. I believe horse-flesh also materially assists German sausages: it keeps them hard.[3]

Attempts in the 1860s to popularize horsemeat, *chevaline*, in England did not work (the French, at the time, fed donkeys, horses and mules to the poor).[4] Lombard *salumi equini della Valchiavenna* is salt-dried horsemeat in hog casings, in which the curing salt is mixed with bay leaves, black pepper, garlic and juniper berries. *Salame d'asino* is still occasionally made from mule and donkey meat in Piedmont. *Luganega della valle dei Mocheni*, from Trentino-Alto Adige, is mostly pork, but always contains some donkey meat. Vicenza still produces sausages from grey donkeys bred for their meat; the lean flesh is moistened with red wine and pork fat. Montferrat's *muletta* was once made from donkeys, but today only their name remains in this Barbera-marinated pork sausage.

Game

All manner of wild mammals (antelope, bison, elk, kangaroo, rabbit), birds (duck, emu, goose, ostrich, pheasant) and reptiles (alligator, snake, turtle) have found their way into sausage casings. Venison sausages are a popular way of using the trimmings of game collected by hunters in the USA. In Europe, it is less common, although one can sometimes find *salame di capriolo* or *salame di cervo* in Piedmont. Livering was an Elizabethan game pudding that made use of offal that would otherwise spoil (it was known as *pwdinen afu* in Wales). Wild boar, *cinghiale*, is a speciality around Siena, in Tuscany, but the Piedmontese make *salame di cinghiale* as well.

Salame from Siena, made with wild boar and moistened with Barolo.

Sandwich shop in Siena. Wild boar, *cinghiale*, is the signature meat in Tuscany, appearing – as in this window – in sausages and hams.

In South Africa, the Dutch-inspired *boerewors* is sometimes made of other available meats, such as antelope, kudu and springbok, or mixtures of meats that are simply labelled 'game sausage'. Canadian brawn (headcheese) uses indigenous game, such as caribou and moose.

Sheep

Brescia's *salsiccia di castrato ovino* contains mutton mixed with veal and pork. Its boiled meats are chilled and de-fatted, then pork fat, garlic, salt, pepper and various herbs and spices are added before the mixture is finely minced and stuffed into hog casings. Abruzzese *salame di pecora* is 90 per cent mutton, with just a little pork. Piedmont's unusual *salame di camoscio* is made from the finely minced tender skin of lambs.

Poultry

The French *saucisse de canard*, or duck sausage, is often garnished with green peppercorns. In the 1970s, duck sausage was a fixture of trendy upscale restaurants – back when raspberry vinegar, pink peppercorns and kiwis were culinary fads. Today, health concerns have made chicken and turkey sausages popular, but in fact poultry has long found its way into sausage casings. *Salame d'oca di Mortara* is a Lombard speciality, made with a mixture of pork and goose. Italian Jews commonly made sausages with goose instead of pork, adapting standard recipes – such as sausage risotto – to suit their needs.

Duck sausage at market day in Foix, France.

Seafood

Any kind of seafood can be made into sausage. However, because most fish and shellfish lack the myosin found in pork, salt alone will not produce a smooth, firm product. Also, the fats in fish either taste too strong or melt away too easily. Usually a panada of breadcrumbs and cream solves both problems. Western seafood sausages tend to use bland, white-fleshed fish (such as sole or haddock) for the primary forcemeat, then garnish with shellfish (crayfish, lobster, scallops or prawn) or pieces of brightly coloured salmon. Seasoning is often delicate, as garlic and chillies could easily overpower the subtle flavours of fish, although an American exception is the Cajun-inspired sausages of Louisiana.

In Korea's Gangwon province, chopped fresh squid make *ojingeo sundae*, while dried squid go into *mareun ojingeo sundae*, and Alaskan pollack fill *myeongtae sundae*.

Vegetables

We tend to think of sausages as being quintessentially 'meaty', but many contain significant amounts of plant matter. They are not necessarily vegan 'not dogs' or imitation sausages made of soy (tofu and texturized vegetable protein, or TVP) and/or gluten (seitan). Some of these ingredients serve only as garnishes, like the pistachios in *mortadella* or the pimento-stuffed olives in olive loaf. In some sausages, herbs and spices are the primary ingredients, and are often used to extend meagre supplies of meat (just as many sausages were created in the first place).

Welsh Glamorgan sausages contain no meat, but are not for vegans, since their protein comes from cheese. Some vegetarian Scottish white puddings are mostly oatmeal, onions, spices and vegetable fat. Seasoned sticky (short-grain or glutinous) rice fills Chinese *nuomi chang*. Inquisition-era Portuguese Jews made something that *looked* like pork sausage, but actually contained no meat: *farinheira* was mostly wheat flour, fat and seasonings (modern versions contain pork and paprika, and closely resemble *chouriço*). It was a fifteenth-century version of 'trying to pass'. It would be interesting to know if it fooled any inquisitors.

Green cabbage leaves mixed with pork meat and fat fill Piedmont's *salcicca di cavolo* or *saucissa d'coi*, while Lombard *salame alle rape* moistens cabbage and turnips with pork fat. Tyrolean *banale ciuighe*, or *coiga*, is an economical smoked salame in which pork is stretched with turnip.

Saumagen is a haggis-like German sausage, in which pork (and sometimes beef) is bulked out with carrots and potatoes, seasoned with allspice, basil, bay leaves, caraway, cardamom, cloves, coriander, garlic, parsley and thyme, then stuffed into a sow's stomach.

Unusual Casings

Just as various starches have been made into wrappers for other foods around the world (dumplings, ravioli, wontons, empanadas, and so on), many different materials have served as containers for encased meats. Tube-shaped hog intestines were clearly a first choice, and still are, but there are other suitable candidates. The small intestines of sheep are also familiar, as the 'little links' of American breakfast sausage, and French *saucisses à la chipolata*.

Sometimes the casings themselves add flavour. The intestines used for *Conca Casale signora*, from Isernia, are washed with lemon juice before being stuffed. Uzbek *piyozli kazy* are made from sheep's lungs and intestines. In Marche, leftover pieces of intestine (chitterlings, or chittlins, in the USA) are pickled in vinegar, basil, bay leaves, fennel seeds and orange peel. The resulting *ciarimbolo* is considered a special treat, and is often consumed by the sausage-makers themselves. Near Rome, *mazzi* – strips of raw pig intestine – are pickled in a mixture

Salame cotto, a mixture of beef and pork, stuffed in a beef bung.

of black and red pepper, *finocchiella* (sweet cicely, *Myrrhis odorata*), garlic, salt and white wine, and then dried or smoked (the latter are known as *mazzi sfumati*). Pickled intestines are sometimes stuffed with pork and caul fat, and dried to make *mazzi ripieni*.

Downstream from the common hog casings, we find the rectum, or bung. Bungs are known, in parts of Italy, as *culari*. Mexican *obispos* – Spanish for 'cardinal's hat' – are haggis-like sausages, with chorizo and offal stuffed into hog bungs. *Culatello* – a crudely affectionate name, something along the lines of 'little anus' – is hog's thigh meat, salted and seasoned, stuffed into a porcine bladder and left to cure in Emilia-Romagna's spore-laden air. Piedmontese *paletta* is brined pork, sweetened with spices and berries, and stuffed into a pig's bladder. *Capocollo*, from several Italian provinces, is packed into pig's bladder as well.

It seems ridiculously obvious, but stomachs make perfect food containers. Like intestines, they frequently serve as casings. The Scottish national dish, haggis, is nothing more than a large sausage made of seasoned sheep organ meats – including but not limited to liver and lungs – bulked out frugally with oats, stuffed into the sheep's stomach. Pig's stomachs have also served as sausage casings, for English yrchins or urchins (slivered almonds provided their hedgehog-like appearance) and Hungarian *töltött malac gyomor*, which is stuffed with a forcemeat of pig head, including skin, cheeks and tongue, and the meat of a few knuckles, seasoned with garlic, pepper and the ever-present paprika.[5] *Bisecon*, a Piedmontese brawn-like salame, is cooked with carrots and celery, then stuffed into the stomach of a pig, as is *garfagna biroldo*, a Tuscan synthesis of blood sausage and brawn, spiced with cinnamon and nutmeg. The spicy Croatian version is *svargl*, while the Serbian equivalent is *pihtije*.

For the Italian *collo di locio ripieno*, the Polish *gęsia szyjka faszerowana* and the Spanish *cuello de ganso relleno*, the skins from the necks of geese are carefully rolled away from the flesh and bones, then filled with various seasoned forcemeats.

Monastero di Vasco and Monregalese have a sausage named, like that of the Umbrians, 'donkey's balls' – in their dialect, *bale d'aso* – that once actually contained donkey meat. Today it is simply beef and pork, seasoned with herbs, nutmeg and red wine, sewn into an oblong pocket of beef tripe.

Occasionally, the stomach – as casing – also provides the protein in the sausage. German *Saumagen* contains some pork or beef, but the bulk of the filling is onions, potatoes and other vegetables, heavily flavoured with marjoram and nutmeg.

Perhaps the ultimate use of an animal's stomach was that of an elephant, as reported by the African explorer Francis Galton in the mid-nineteenth century:

> The dish called *beatee* is handy to make. It is a kind of haggis made with blood, a good quantity of fat shred small, some of the tenderest of the flesh, together with the heart and lungs of the animal, cut or torn into small shivers, all of which is put into the stomach and roasted, by being suspended before the fire with a string . . . It is a most delicious morsel, even without pepper, salt, or any seasoning.[6]

Omentum or caul fat (*crépine*) is a lacy tissue surrounding and supporting the abdominal organs. It traps fat between its layers, making it an ideal material for wrapping sausages. As they cook the fat melts out, keeping the meat moist, while the thin but strong membrane holds the forcemeat together. The French sometimes refer to sausage wrapped in caul fat as *coiffes*. *Crépinettes* are flat patties of sausage meat wrapped in caul fat; *gayettes* are similar, but spherical. *Attereaux* are

A chef at Le Cordon Bleu holds up an omentum, the caul fat that covers some of the pig's internal organs.

gayettes of paprika- and vinegar-seasoned pork neck meat and liver, bound with egg. Provençal pork *caillettes* contain bread, egg, greens, garlic, onions and parsley. *Seftali kebabi* – grilled cylindrical sausages of lamb, onion and parsley, wrapped in caul fat – are Cypriot favourites. Other caul fat-wrapped types include bullet-shaped *boulettes* and Welsh faggots (which are round, like *gayettes*).

This style of sausage has a long history. Platina, in the fifteenth century, gave a recipe for *escium ex iecore* (liver sausages containing cheese, egg, raisins, parsley and marjoram) wrapped in caul fat.[7] Piedmont's *gayettes* and *frisse e grive* are filled with liver and lung.

Apicius offered a recipe for a blood sausage stuffed into a pig's uterus. Some 600 years later, Constantine Porphyrogenitus of Byzantium (the fourth emperor of the Macedonian dynasty) wrote *De ceremoniis*, a book that outlined the duties of everyone in the court. It required his kitchens to provide sausages made of 'wombs and nerves' (we do not know – or want to know, in anything other than a purely academic sense – what was meant by 'nerves' in the tenth century). Calves' udders still encase finely minced fish or meat in Polish *kromeskis*. They are sometimes wrapped, instead, with bacon, dipped in batter and deep-fried.

Cou d'oie or *cou de canard* are sausage-stuffed skins from the necks of geese or ducks. In Piedmont, the neck skin is similarly stuffed with goose meat and fat to make *collo d'oca*, while their *salame d'oca* may be stitched into the rest of the goose's skin. In *helzel*, or 'false *kishka*', a chicken's neck skin is stuffed with a seasoned paste of flour.

Sewn pig's head skin encloses *salame di testa* from Ossola in Piedmont, and Ligurian *testa in cassetta*, while various kinds of *zampone* are stuffed into the skin of a pig's trotters. The skin of the entire hock and lower part of a pig's leg serves as

Zampino – the same forcemeat as *zampone*, but stuffed into sewn pig skin instead of the traditional trotter.

casing (once stitched tightly) for Ligurian *gambetto di maiale*, a cinnamon- and nutmeg-flavoured sausage of pork and blood.

Squids' bodies also make perfect casings, and many stuffed squid recipes qualify as sausages. Pork and cellophane noodles seasoned with pepper and salty *nuoc mam* (fish sauce) fill Vietnamese *muc nhoi thit*. Spanish cooks stuff *calamares rellenos con morcilla* with blood sausage, a delight in black and white. The air bladder of a croaker – a fish of the *Sciaenidae* family – provides the casing for Korean *eogyo sundae*.

Sausage casings need not be animal in origin; plant materials work too. In El Salvador, *chorizo Salvadoreño* is wrapped in corn husks, like *tamales* (but without the polenta-like *masa* found in Mexican *tamales*). They are tied to form small links 5 cm (2 in.) long. Vietnamese *giò lụa*, also known as *chà lụa* (pork pounded until completely smooth, bound with potato starch, and seasoned with pepper, sugar and the omnipresent *nuoc mam*), are wrapped tightly in banana leaves, then boiled for an hour or so. After the Vietnam War, immigrants in America

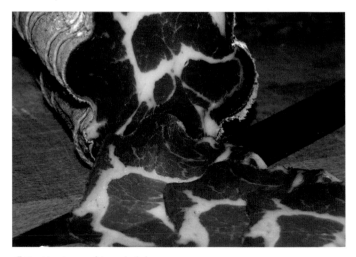

Coppa picante, cured in a cloth bag.

A string of *nem ninh hoa*, Vietnamese sausages wrapped in banana leaves.

began substituting aluminium foil for the traditional – and hard to get – banana leaves. In the USA, muslin bags (sometimes impregnated with black pepper) are used to contain Virginia's 'cloth bologna' while it is cooked and smoked. The steamed pudding bags used in English cooking probably suggested them, or perhaps those used to protect curing hams from insects.

Unusual Binding Agents

Salt may be an essential part of sausage – it certainly is in a linguistic sense – but not all sausages are bound together by soluble myosin. Catalonian *boudin* (known as *botifarra negra*) and Louisiana's *boudin rouge* (a descendent of French *boudin noir*) are, in part, blood sausages, but their primary protein is muscle tissue, and blood is used only as a binding agent.

In Islamic countries, lambs replace pigs as grist for sausage. However, lamb does not form the binding myosin as well as pork, which leads to a crumbly texture, so the albumen in eggs is sometimes used to provide a smooth matrix. Alternatively, starch can serve the same purpose.

A panada is a binding agent for sausage that makes use of the starch-thickening properties of cereal grains. A paste of some form of grain (such as breadcrumbs, flour or meal) moistened with a liquid (cream, milk, stock or wine) can sometimes serve the same function as dissolved protein. The oats in haggis could be considered a form of panada, while Pennsylvania Dutch scrapple uses cornmeal. German *Balkenbrij* is sometimes bound with barley, while the Dutch version contains wheat flour or oats. Various starches bind Piedmontese blood puddings: *sanginaccio con pane* has stale bread; *marzapane*, breadcrumbs; *sanginaccio con patate*, potatoes; and *sanginaccio con riso*, rice.

Delicate mousses of seafood or poultry may be bound and lightened with whipped egg whites. Albumen, after all, is a liquid protein until it is cooked. Souse, or brawn, is a kind of sausage in which chunks of meat are held together in a stiff matrix of pork stock that has been reduced into a sliceable jelly. When meats – especially those rich in connective tissue – are simmered for a long time in water, their collagen dissolves to form liquid gelatine that sets upon cooling. If the gelatine content of the broth is high enough, it forms a firm aspic-like matrix to support those scraps of cooked meat. Brawn – in common with any dish containing aspic – is always served cold, as its binding gelatine melts when heated.

Gentrification of the Humble Sausage

The very word 'humble' suggests an origin in 'umbles', the innards or organ meats that were not prized by the rich, and therefore became peasant food. They were, originally, nothing more than a way to use all parts of an animal, and extend its shelf life – essentially, a way to maximize meat and meat by-products as part of rural cookery. We know the ancients were familiar with sausages, and that they had already moved to the tables of the rich by the time of Apicius. During the Renaissance, Europeans rediscovered the favourite dishes of their ancestors. *Mortadella*, already a well-known regional speciality, received a laurel-leaf garland from Platina in the fifteenth century, when he associated it with the *insicia* of ancient Rome. Ludovicus Nonnius, writing a century later in France, said: 'I see that pork is preferred in our age to other meats. When enclosed in an intestine casing with fat and condiments, the sausages are considered delicacies.'[8] He almost seemed surprised that sausages had become a gourmet treat in themselves.

Cassoulet, a typical stew of southern France.

Simple dishes, such as the French *cassoulet* and *choucroute garnie*, and Brazilian *feijoada* – peasant foods, designed to be filling, cheap and flavourful – became the classics of international cuisine. Pork, and especially pork sausage, has long been the star of dishes that peasants filled out with inexpensive ingredients like cabbage and beans. In addition to those already mentioned, there is Spanish *fabada asturiana*, with large dried white beans called *fabes de la Granja*. It includes chorizo (and/or *longaniza*) and *morcilla*, plus bacon and saffron. In another Spanish peasant dish, *olla podrida*, sausage and beans (or chickpeas) are cooked so slowly that they can barely be distinguished from each other – hence the name, which means 'rotten pot'.

Conclusion

The lowly sausage, once no more than the efficient use of every part of a slaughtered beast, has evolved into the darling of diners – daring and otherwise – around the world. H. L. Mencken, whose love-hate relationship with hot dogs was often displayed in the press, once wished that the ordinary wiener could be more like other sausages, 'for there are more different sausages in Germany than there are breakfast foods in America, and if there is a bad one among them then I have never heard of it'.[1]

After ecstatically describing the range of sizes, shapes, textures and flavours available in encased meats, Mencken wrote prophetically:

> There should be dogs for all appetites, all tastes, all occasions. They should come in rolls of every imaginable kind and accompanied by every sort of relish from Worcestershire sauce to chutney . . . The hot dog should be elevated to the level of an art form.

This hot-dog manifesto was published in the *Baltimore Sun* on 4 November 1929. Had Mencken lived long enough, he would have seen the level of artistry of all sausages (not just

A 1950s ad for what at the time was one of the largest sausage companies in the u.s. The original British company was founded in 1827. Note the 'pigs-in-a-blanket', popular in Denmark, the u.s., Great Britain, the Netherlands and Russia. Naming variations include the German 'sausage in a dressing gown' and the Israeli 'Moses in the Ark'.

'Gourmet' dogs at Hot Doug's, in Chicago, Illinois. Top: grilled alligator hot dog with smoked gouda. Bottom: classic Chicago dog with all the trimmings, but substituting deep fried Cajun andouille for the more prosaic – but still good – Vienna beef.

hot dogs) increase exponentially. Today, sausages are equally at home in street vendors' carts and in white-tablecloth dining establishments. The hot dog itself has bloomed in places like Chicago (where it is taken very seriously). Establishments like Franks 'n' Dawgs and Hot Doug's offer a constantly changing and seemingly endless set of variations on the theme of encased meats. What is best about this phenomenon is that – for all its inventiveness and sophistication – no one forgets this basic truth: sausages are the food of the people, inexpensive, delicious and just plain fun to eat. Anywhere, anyhow, anytime.

Recipes

Basic Sausage

This is the simplest possible recipe, the starting point for any kind of sausage. You need only decide on the kind of protein, seasoning, texture, size, casing or no casing, smoking or not, fresh or dried, fermented or not – there are infinite variations!
Makes 2.25 kg (5 lb)

1.8 kg (4 lb) meat, fish or poultry
450 g (1 lb) firm fat (pork or beef), chilled until almost frozen
25 g (1 oz) kosher or sea salt
herbs or spices of your choice
casings, if desired, soaked and well rinsed

Cut the meat and fat into 25-mm (1-in.) cubes, discarding any pieces of gristle or bone. Mix it with the salt and your chosen seasoning in a non-reactive bowl, cover and chill in the refrigerator for at least 4 hours or overnight. Chill the mincer at the same time.

Mince or chop the meat to your desired texture. Mix the mince if it has not become sticky (this is often unnecessary if the meat has rested with salt long enough, since passage through the mincer mixes it sufficiently to bind the sausage).

Stuff the sausage, or form into patties. If using the sausage fresh, refrigerate until ready to cook. Otherwise, wrap tightly in pre-portioned packages of cling film and freeze, or continue with additional processes (such as drying, smoking or curing, which may require the use of curing agents and/or preservatives).

Italian Sausage, *Salsiccia*

This is a simple variation on the method and ingredients for Basic Sausage.
Makes 2.5 kg (5 lb)

2.25 kg (5 lb) Basic Sausage (see above)
15 g (½ oz) freshly ground black pepper
25 g (1 oz) fennel seeds
½ tsp crushed chilli (hot red pepper) flakes

Add the additional seasonings to the basic recipe with the salt, then proceed as normal. For a hot version, also add 1 tsp cayenne and 2 tsp paprika.

Louisiana Andouille

This sausage has little to do with its Old World namesake, other than the fact that the ancestors of today's Cajuns came from Normandy (where French *andouille* was popular) via Nova Scotia. Cajun *andouille* is always smoked, but this recipe provides two alternatives for cooks who do not have access to a smoker.
Makes 2.25 kg (5 lb)

2.25 kg (5 lb) fatty pork shoulder
25 g (1 oz) kosher or sea salt
1 large garlic clove, minced
½ tsp ground white pepper
¾ tsp mixed ground spices (allspice, ancho chilli, cayenne, clove and nutmeg)
¾ tsp dried thyme
1½ tbsp paprika (or smoked paprika; see below)

Cut the meat and fat into 25-mm (1-in.) cubes, discarding any pieces of gristle or bone. Mix it with the salt, garlic and seasoning in a non-reactive bowl, cover and chill in the refrigerator for at least 4 hours or overnight. Chill the mincer at the same time.

Mince the meat using the coarse plate. Mix the mince mixture until it starts to become sticky, fry a small piece and adjust the seasoning if necessary.

Stuff the sausage, twist into 20-cm (8-in.) links (twisting in the opposite direction each time) and hang to dry in the refrigerator until the pellicle has formed. Hot-smoke (74–85°C/165–85°F) for 4–5 hours.

If you are not using a smoker, the drying step can be omitted. Add ¼ tsp liquid smoke to the minced meat, mix thoroughly then fry a small piece to check the flavour, adding more liquid smoke if desired. Alternatively, if you substitute smoked paprika, hot smoking and liquid smoke are not required. Unsmoked *andouille*, obviously, will not have the dry surface or dark colour of the smoked version.

If using the sausage fresh, refrigerate until ready to cook. Otherwise, wrap it tightly in pre-portioned packages of cling film and freeze, or continue with additional processes (like drying, smoking or curing, which may require the use of curing agents and/or preservatives).

Lamb Loukaniko

This savoury sausage highlights the Greek taste for anise flavours, and the savoury flavour of foods cooked on the grill. A sunny day, ice-cold ouzo, some pitta bread and a salad of chickpeas and red onion (see below) make for a great picnic.

680 g (1 ½ lb) lamb
225 g (½ lb) pork fat
25 g (¼ cup) grated Kefalotyri cheese
1 tbsp grated orange zest
1 tbsp anise or fennel seeds

15 g (½ oz) kosher salt
1 tbsp flat-leaf parsley
ground black pepper and chilli flakes, to taste
120 ml (¼ cup) dry rosé wine (such as Roditis), ice-cold

Chop the lamb and pork fat into 25-mm (1-in.) pieces, and chill. Combine the next six ingredients; add to the lamb and pork fat, mix well, cover and chill overnight. Chill the mincer and bowl at the same time.

Next day, add the wine to the seasoned meat. Mix well, then mince coarsely into the chilled bowl. Mix until the meat becomes sticky, then stuff into casings or wrap in caul fat. Grill until well done, and serve hot.

Serves 4

Chickpea Salad

1 can chickpeas, drained and rinsed
1 small red onion, chopped
1 cucumber, peeled, seeded and diced
1 ripe tomato, seeded and diced
120 ml (½ cup) kalamata olives, stoned
½ tsp dried oregano
60 ml (¼ cup) olive oil
1 tbsp freshly squeezed lemon juice
1 tbsp chopped flat-leaf parsley
kosher or sea salt and black pepper, to taste

Combine all the ingredients except the parsley in a non-reactive bowl, and season. Cover and set aside (do not put in the refrigerator, or the tomatoes will lose their flavour). Just before serving, put the salad on a wide decorative plate, using a slotted spoon and discarding the excess liquid that will have accumulated. Garnish with the parsley.

Serves 4

Linguiça

This is a modern Portuguese version of an ancient Roman sausage.
Makes 2.25 kg (5 lb)

1.4 kg (3 lb) lean boneless pork shoulder
900 g (2 lb) pork fat, chilled until almost frozen
3 garlic cloves, peeled and minced
1 tbsp paprika
25 g (1 oz) kosher salt
½ tsp ground cinnamon
½ tsp ground allspice
1 tbsp crushed chilli (hot red pepper) flakes
60 ml (¼ cup) red wine vinegar
1 tbsp ground coriander seeds
120 ml (½ cup) iced water

Cut the pork into 25-mm (1-in.) cubes and mince it finely. Cut the pork fat into 25-mm (1-in.) cubes, mince it coarsely and add it to the pork mince. Combine the minced meats with all the remaining ingredients, then mix until sticky. Cover and chill for 4 hours or overnight.

Stuff into hog casings, pricking any air pockets with a needle. Form single 'links' of about 50 cm (18 in.), and tie into loops, like a *kielbasa*. Use immediately, or package and freeze in the usual manner.

Quick Mexican Chorizo

Traditionally, chorizo would develop its tangy flavour through fermentation with *Lactobacillus*. This recipe avoids risk for home cooks, and is ready to use much sooner.
Makes 4 225-g (½-lb) portions

900 g (2 lb) pork shoulder (20 per cent fat)
3 tbsp chilli powder

1 tbsp cayenne
3 large garlic cloves, minced
3 tbsp dried oregano
1 tsp freshly ground black pepper
1 tsp cinnamon
2 tsp freshly ground cumin seeds
15 g (½ oz) kosher or sea salt
90 ml (3 fl. oz) red wine vinegar
90 ml (3 fl. oz) iced water

Cut the pork into 25-mm (1-in.) pieces, cover and chill. Combine with the next eight ingredients, mix well, cover and chill overnight. Chill the mincer and bowl at the same time.

Next day, add the vinegar and iced water to the pork mixture. Mix well, then mince coarsely into the chilled bowl. Mix until sticky, form into 225-g (½-lb) patties, seal each tightly in cling film and cure in the refrigerator for three days before cooking or freezing in labelled freezer bags.

Queso Fundido

This dish, also known as *choriqueso*, is a popular hangover cure in Mexico, possibly because it is easy to make when even the slightest effort seems unbearable. However, no prior overindulgence is required to enjoy it.

The roasted strips of poblano chilli are known as *rajas* (a small factoid, useful if you feel the need to show off to other foodies).

1 fresh poblano chilli (see note below)
1 tbsp olive oil (not extra virgin)
225 g (½ lb) Quick Mexican Chorizo (see above), crumbled
340 g (¾ lb) queso Oaxaca, grated (or shredded mozzarella)
salt, to taste
tortilla chips, for dipping

Preheat the oven to 175°C (350°F). Roast the chilli over an open flame until charred all over. Place in a bag to steam for a few minutes, to loosen the skin. Remove from the bag and rub off the blackened skin, then cut in half lengthways and remove the stem and seeds. Slice crossways into strips 6 mm (¼ in.) wide, and set aside.

Heat the oil in a cast-iron frying pan until almost smoking. Add the chorizo and fry, breaking up any large pieces, until completely cooked. Taste for seasoning, adding salt if desired. Spread the cooked chorizo out in an ovenproof dish (see note below), top with the poblano strips (*rajas*) and grated cheese, and bake until the cheese is melted. Serve with tortilla chips.

Note: If you are preparing this as a cure for your *own* hangover, feel free to substitute the milder strips of canned green chilli. That way you needn't risk dealing with an open flame and sharp knife. Also, you can reuse the same pan to finish the dish (provided it has an ovenproof handle), to save you searching for a new one. Really – how concerned do want you be about how things look the morning after?

Serves 4 (as a starter)

Merguez

This is the classic spicy-hot lamb sausage from Tunisia. It is characterized by a typically Islamic complex spice mixture, a hint of fruit and – for obvious reasons – no pork.
Makes 2.25 kg (5 lb)

2.25 kg (5 lb) fatty lamb trimmings
25 g (1 oz) kosher or sea salt
2 tbsp paprika
1 tbsp cracked black pepper
2 tsp ground cumin
2 tsp cayenne
2 tsp minced garlic
1½ tsp ground cinnamon

1 ½ tsp ground ginger
1 ½ tsp thyme leaves
180 ml (6 fl. oz) pomegranate juice

Cut any large chunks of meat and fat into pieces no bigger than 25 mm (1 in.), trimming and discarding any pieces of gristle, sinew or bone. Toss the meat with the salt and all the remaining ingredients (except the pomegranate juice) in a non-reactive bowl, cover and chill in the refrigerator for at least 4 hours or overnight. Chill the mincer at the same time.

Mince the meat coarsely. Stir in the juice and mix until it starts to become sticky. Stuff the forcemeat into collagen casings, and twist into 125-mm (5-in.) lengths. If using the sausage fresh, refrigerate until ready to cook. Otherwise, wrap tightly in pre-portioned packages of cling film and freeze.

Orecchiette with Broccoli Rabe and Sausage

Orecchiette ('little ears') are a favourite form of pasta in Apulia, the 'heel' of Italy's boot. Some purists object to the inclusion of sausage in this dish, but the sweetness of the pork provides a lovely counterpoint to the bitter greens.

1 large bunch broccoli rabe (rapini), rinsed and chopped
3 tbsp olive oil
4 garlic cloves, chopped
½ tsp crushed chilli (red pepper) flakes
2.3 kg (1 lb) Italian Sausage, as above, crumbled
450 g (1 lb) dried *orecchiette*, or medium pasta shells
salt and pepper, to taste
grated Pecorino Romano cheese, to serve

In a large pot of salted water, cook the broccoli rabe until bright green. Shock the greens by placing them in a bowl of iced water, but do not discard the cooking water.

Sauté the garlic and chilli flakes in olive oil, until the garlic just begins to colour. Add the sausage and begin to cook, stirring to brown it evenly. While the sausage is cooking, add the pasta to the broccoli rabe's cooking water and cook until almost done (it will finish cooking in the sauce).

When the sausage is browned, add the blanched and drained broccoli rabe to the pan, and heat through. Add the nearly cooked pasta to the sausage and greens and toss until tender and well-coated. You may need to moisten the mixture with a little of the cooking water. Toss to finish cooking the pasta in the sauce.

Taste for seasoning, and serve with grated Pecorino cheese on the table.

Serves 4

Appendix: A Selection of Regional Sausages

Italy

Every part of Italy has its own specialities; this is just a sampling of sausages from the various provinces.

The Abruzzese are fond of liver, and produce two very different sausages from it: *fegato pazzo* and *fegato dolce*. The former – 'crazy liver' – is spiked with hot red chilli; the latter is sweetened with honey and smoked. *Fiaschetta aquilana* is pressed into a flattened pear (or 'flask') shape. *Coglioni di mulo* (or *mortadella di campotosto*) resembles neither other *coglioni* nor *mortadella*; a square garnish of *lardo* runs down the centre, and every round slice has a white square in the middle. *Ventricina vastese*, spiked with chilli, is redolent of the local wild fennel, while *ventricina di Guilmi* contains fragrant orange peel.

From Apulia, *cervellata Pugliese* is a fresh sausage of beef, goat, mutton or veal (or some combination) with basil, garlic and a sharp, dry cheese. It is stuffed into a continuous length of sheep casings and coiled, not formed into links. The short, plump, fresh links of *salsiccia salentina o di Lecce* are seasoned with lemon zest and moistened with white wine. Smoked *salsiccia Pugliese* is studded with peppercorns and fennel seeds; *sanguinacci di Lecce*, a savoury blood pudding, contains brains and aromatic herbs; and slender *zampitti* contain lamb, pork or veal, liberally spiced with red chilli and stuffed into sheep casings.

Curiously, no sausages made in Basilicata (Lucania) are called *lucanica* or *luganega*. *Salsicca pezzente* or *pezzente Basilicata* ('beggar's sausage'), stuffed with scraps and offal not used for more expensive sausages, comes heavily spiced with fennel seeds and red chilli.

Calabrese culinary traditions are a fusion of Greek, Roman and Arabic influences, with a generous helping of New World ingredients, including tomatoes and chillies. Their *cervellata* scorches with red chilli, as does *salciccia di Calabria*, which is smoked before curing. *'Nduja* is also laced with chillies, but is made with pork liver, lungs and plenty of soft, spreadable fat – an Italian take on the German *Braunschweiger*.

From Campania, fresh *cervellatina* ('small brain sausage') does not actually contain brains, although it probably did in the ancient past; today, it is spiked with hot red chilli. Campania's *mozzariello* sounds like stretchy cheese, but is a spicy Neapolitan pork sausage.

In Emilia-Romagna, Bologna's *mortadella* has been justifiably famous at least since the fourteenth century (a recipe for it appeared in the *Libro di Cucina del Secolo XIV*, or Book of Cooking of the Fourteenth Century). Its smooth forcemeat is garnished with cubes of white pork fat and, sometimes, pistachios. Piacenza's *Mariola* gets its faintly musky aroma from mushrooms. Ferrara's *salama da sugo* begins like *capocolla*, but adds liver, tongue and two kinds of fat: *pancetta* (belly) and *lardo di gola* (neck), sprinkled with red wine, sweet cinnamon and cloves. *Ciavàr* (or *salsiccia matta*, 'crazy sausage') – Sangiovese-infused pork and offal, wrapped in caul fat – is available fresh or preserved in olive oil.

Salsiccia, fresh sausage in hog casings.

The alpine and sub-alpine region of Friuli-Venezia Giulia has culinary traditions that are unlike stereotypical 'Italian food'. Its location suggests its affinity with the Austrian and eastern Slavic kitchens. *Cevapici* is made of beef, pork and lamb, spiked with chilli. *Marcundela*, a mixture of pig's offal (spleen, kidneys, liver and lungs) flavoured with garlic and wine, is wrapped in caul fat. Friulian *musetto* contains mildly seasoned pork from the head and shins, with cinnamon, cloves and coriander seeds.

From Lazio, Roman pork is more likely to be found as ham or bacon, although some ends up in sausage. The recipe for *Viterbo susianella* – which lists heart, liver, pancreas, *pancetta*, *guanciale* (cured, unsmoked bacon made from the pig's cheeks, rubbed with sage) and offal – is said to date back to Etruscan times (although the absence of contemporary written records and the inclusion of post-Etruscan-era red pepper does not suggest historical accuracy). *Mortadellina amatriciana* is a lightly smoked version of the classic Bolognese sausage, garnished with a square strip of fat running down its centre. *Salsiccia di Monte San Biagio* – fresh sausage links flavoured with New World chillies, and coriander, orange peel and raisins – reveals a culinary connection to the Islamic Middle East. *Salsicce sott'olio* is sold in jars, seasoned with garlic, fennel, nutmeg and red chilli, then air-dried before completing its cure under oil.

The Ligurians are a thrifty people; they make *frizze* (patties of pork offal and juniper berries, tightly wrapped in caul fat) and *mostardella*, coarse salame made of whatever scraps of pork are left after making other sausages. More extravagant is *salamino di animelle e sangue di maiale*, fresh sausage of pig's blood and thymus glands (sweetbreads), made with milk, cooked onions and pine nuts.

'Drunken' *coppa ciochetùna* from Lombardy is marinated in red wine, garlic, salt and spices before being stuffed into hog casings. *Cotecotto* is a pre-cooked sausage, usually made from pork, but sometimes beef or horseflesh. The local variation of *luganega*, made near Milan, is *luganega di Monza*, fortified with Marsala wine and Grana Padano cheese.

In Marche, *ciauscolo* is a soft, spreadable paste of pork fat and trimmings, lightly smoked and flavoured with garlic and juniper berries, and sweetened with *vincotto*, syrupy reduced grape must (juice). Its name comes from an ancient Roman word for an appetizer or snack. Too rich (as much as 50 per cent fat) to eat in large portions, it is smeared on bread like a canapé. While most Italians prepare *coppa* with the excellent meat found in the 'cape' of the pig, the salumeria of southern Marche make their traditional *coppa di Ascoli Piceno* from a mixture of odds and ends. Cartilage, ears, skin, snout and tongue are boiled, flavoured with cinnamon, garlic and nutmeg, and garnished with almonds, pistachios and walnuts. *Coppa di testa* uses all the scraps of meat from the pig's head – everything but the skull and brain. It is not cubed (as in brawn), so cross sections of ears are plainly visible in this rolled assemblage. Fortunately, it is well-flavoured with orange peel and lemon juice. *Mazzafegati* are liver sausages: a savoury one made with pine nuts, and a sweet one with added orange zest and sugar (available fresh or cured). Fresh coarsely ground *salsiccia tradizionale di Fabriano* is beef and *pancetta* infused with garlic.

From Molise, spreadable *ventricina di Montenero di Bisaccia* is made of pork leg meat, combined with fat, fennel flowers and paprika, stuffed into a pig's bladder, coated with melted fat and left to age for a year. *Salsicce di fegato di Rionero Sannitico* – mostly lean pork, with fat and offal (not just liver, as the name suggests), seasoned with chilli and garlic – is briefly dried then preserved under a layer of lard.

Doganeghin (beef) and *luganeghin* (phonetically linked to *luganica*) are generic names for sausage in Piedmont. Their *mortadella, mortadella di fegato cotta*, comes from Novara. Smaller than that of Bologna, it is cured, rather than being cooked; *fidighin* is the smoked version. In 1848, the pre-unification Albertino Statute made an exception to the rule that sausages must contain pork, allowing the region to produce *salsiccia di Bra*, made entirely of beef, to be sold in a nearby Jewish community. Today the sausage usually contains some pork fat. *Gavi testa in cassetta* is a kind of brawn that includes beef heart and lean pork, seasoned with red chilli, garnished with pine nuts. Turin's *Valli Valdesi mustardela* is Piedmont's blood sausage; its sweet-sour taste comes from cinnamon, cloves and nutmeg.

In Sardinia, pressed brawn-like *testa in cassetta* gets some additional texture from bits of the pig's skin. Seasoned with lemon zest, nutmeg, pepper and strong alcohol (grappa or whiskey), it is always eaten fresh.

Many Sicilian pigs forage for acorns and berries, giving them lean, deep-flavoured flesh. Sausages have probably been made on the island since the Greeks first arrived, more than 3,000 years ago. The Sicilians' love affair with pork was interrupted briefly, from the ninth to the eleventh century, when Muslims occupied the island, and Arabic taste still affects Sicilian cooking (cinnamon, oranges, saffron and the combination of pine nuts and raisins are relics of Islamic culinary culture). Typical Sicilian sausages – such as *supprissato di Nicosia* and *u suppessato* – probably began to be made shortly after 1061, when William the Conqueror's cousin Roger I freed the island from the Fatimid caliphate.

Perhaps the best-known Tuscan salame is *finocchiona*. Its signature ingredient is local wild fennel seed, but it also contains long pepper (*Piper longum*) and red wine. Tuscan *testa in cassetta* is quite different from Sardinia's: it lacks lemon zest or alcohol, but adds hot red chilli, rosemary, sweet cinnamon, cloves and mace. It is garnished with pine nuts and chopped sweet red pepper before being simmered in a synthetic casing. *Garfagnana biroldo*, a hybrid of brawn and blood pudding, is lightly seasoned with sweet spices: cinnamon, cloves, nutmeg, star anise and wild fennel. *Mallegato* from Pisa is a more strongly flavoured version. Siena's blood pudding is *buristo*, a dark, smooth-textured sausage, garnished with large chunks of pure white fat. The word is an Italianate contraction of the German *Blutwurst*; Italy's first king, in the fifth century, was Odoacer, who is described in some accounts as 'Gothic' or German. Tuscans love wild boar, *cinghiale*, and it can be found in salami around the region; San Gimignano's features pine nuts and pistachios.

The Tyrol has foods reminiscent of both Italy and Germany. Its blood sausage, *baldonazzio sanguinaccio* or *brusti*, has a sweet-sour flavour typical of German cooking. The Tyroleans also share the German fondness for smoked meats. *Frankfurter Würstels*, the ancestors of today's hot dogs, have been made of finely minced smoked pork and veal since the thirteenth century. *Probusto*, from Vallagarina, is similar, but seasoned with cinnamon, cloves, mace and paprika.

Kaminwurst, or *salamino affumicato*, gets its German name from the cumin seeds that produce its distinctive taste. Even the fresh sausages of the region, such as *salsicce del Trentino*, incorporate northern tastes – cumin, horseradish and nutmeg.

In Umbria, *coglioni di mulo* ('mule's balls') are medium-sized oval sausages made of pork leg and shoulder meat, along with a garnish of *lardo* – cured and seasoned pork fat.

The food of the cool sub-alpine province of Val d'Aosta reflects that of adjacent France and Switzerland, with lots of game (hence *cacciatore Saouseusse* – 'Swiss hunter's sausage' – and wild-boar salame), dairy foods and more subtle seasonings. Their salami include *bon bocon*, a red wine-infused dry sausage that looks like something one would find in a French market; *boudin salame*, a blood sausage containing cooked potatoes; and tiny *salsicce della Val d'Aosta*, made with cinnamon, nutmeg and wine.

In Veneto, cannonball-shaped *bondiola* is seasoned with red wine, stuffed into a pig's bladder and tied with twine. It is the model for a range of similar local sausages. In *bondiola di Adria*, veal is added to the basic recipe, and there is also a smoked version, *bondiola affumicata*. *Bondiola di Treviso* includes minced bacon rind, and is occasionally garnished with an entire salted pig's tongue. Since the fourteenth century, *luganega di Treviso* has been made with a mixture of cinnamon, cloves, coriander, mace and nutmeg, enriched with finely ground or pounded *pancetta*.

France

The cultural and culinary regions of France do not coincide with modern political boundaries, so it makes more sense to speak of these than of the names on a map.

Bordeaux's tiny *loukanka* is a spicy sausage that is grilled and served with raw oysters at Christmas. From Burgundy, elegant *judru* is flavoured with cognac, nutmeg and truffles; rustic *saucisson de Lyon* is a garlic-laced dried salami, garnished with whole peppercorns.

From Champagne, *andouillette de Troyes*, a coarse-textured sausage of tripe and pork, once contained veal as well (until fear of BSE,

vine spongiform encephalopathy, led to a ban on veal in these
sages). *Boudin blanc de Rethel*, protected under EU law, must con-
n pork, pork and veal, or chicken, as well as eggs and milk, but
) starch whatsoever.

The Provençal *saucisson de taureau* must contain at least 60 per
nt lean meat from the bulls of the marshy plains of the Camargue.
ucisson de Provence*, a dried and smoked sausage containing *quatre
ices* and sugar, is garnished with whole peppercorns, while dried
ucisson d'Arles is just pork and salt.

Alsace-Lorraine has changed hands with Germany many times,
and Germany's influence is revealed in all things culinary, from
the styles of wine to the types of sausage. Alsatian blood sausage,
Schwarzwurst, is a French version of *Blutwurst*. *Saucisses croquantes*,
plump cumin-scented pork and beef sausages, are sometimes
labelled *Knackwurst* in French markets. *Saucisse de Strasbourg*, also
known as *saucisse de Francfort*, is named for one German city, and for
a city in Alsace that has been intermittently in German hands (or
sometimes known as *saucisse allemande*, 'German sausage'). It is

Saucisson de taureau, made from bulls bred for fighting.

another fine-textured sausage, flavoured with coriander, mace and white pepper.

Great Britain

British regional English sausages include Lincolnshire, flavoured with sage and bound with breadcrumbs; Wiltshire, seasoned with mace and sage, or with ginger or parsley; Yorkshire, spiced with cayenne, mace, nutmeg and black pepper; and an unusual one from the West Country that features apple, sage and scrumpy (a strong cider). Cumberland sausage, of coarsely chopped pork seasoned only with black and white pepper, and generally not formed into links, has been a regional speciality for as much as half a millennium, and has since 2011 enjoyed the same level of protected status as Champagne and Parmigiano-Reggiano.

Gloucester Old Spot sausages are not named for the place, but for the breed of pig used. The flesh of free range Old Spots has a higher fat content than modern lean pork, making juicier, more flavourful sausages.

The red puddings of Scotland are thick, un-encased sausage-shaped lumps of seasoned forcemeat (bacon, beef, breadcrumbs, fat and port wine), dipped in batter and deep-fried. An all-pork red pudding comes in a synthetic red casing, and is sliced and fried; it is served with, or in place of, the black pudding in Scottish breakfasts.

Elsewhere in Western Europe

Beginning in the northwest, we see that Iceland has blood sausages (*blóðmör*), plus blood and liver sausages (*slátur*), with high fat contents appropriate to its cold climate. Iceland is not suited to pork production, so its sausages are made mostly from lamb (in *blóðmör*, beef suet is substituted for pork fat). Thick *bjúgu* is made with horse, lamb and a little pork. *Pylsa* is a generic name for sausage in Icelandic, and often refers to their most popular encased meat: hot dogs.

Finnish sausage with mustard – a combination that recognizes no geographic boundaries.

Norwegian *pølse* is another frankfurter-like sausage, while the smoked *julepølse* is plumper, either white or red, and usually served at Christmas. Many Norwegian sausages are heavily smoked and may contain the flesh of goats, horses (*fåremorr, fårepølse, fåresnabb, haugpølse, haugtusse farepølse, sognemorr gilde, sølvfaks stabbur, sognekorv gilde, tiriltunga, toppen, trøndermoor*), lambs or adult sheep, moose or reindeer (*rallarsnabb gilde, reinrose reinsdyr-pølse*). Offal (hearts, livers and lungs) and blood are common ingredients. The Norwegians and Swedes often bulk out their sausages with potatoes (and barley, in Swedish *isterband*).

Generic Swedish sausage, called *korv*, is typically dried (*spickekorv*) or semi-dried (*hashallsmedvurst, isterband, röktmedvurst*). *Falukorv*, a mixture of meats plus potatoes, was invented in Sweden by German workers who immigrated to work in Falun's copper mine, four centuries ago.

Finnish blood sausages (*verimakkara*), such as *mustamakkara*, have been made for more than 400 years. Like most blood puddings, they are bound with grain; in Finland, rye is used. Unlike most blood sausages, they are baked, not boiled, and served with lingonberry preserve. Other Finnish sausages bulk out their forcemeats with potatoes (*perunamakkara*) or barley (*ryynimakkara*).

Lauantaimakkara is a smooth *mortadella*-like sausage that takes its name from a similar French sausage made in Lyon. *Siskonmakkara*, a soft, smooth-textured fresh sausage, is generally crumbled into other dishes (in the same way as Mexican chorizo), rather than being served in its casing. Its name evolved from the French *saucisse*, via a convoluted path through German (*Sausichen*).

Pølse means sausage in Danish as well as Norwegian, and a *pølsevogn* is a Danish street vendor's cart (aptly nicknamed *café fodkoldt* – 'café cold feet'), where one can buy the omnipresent Scandinavian *røde pølser* (hot dogs). *Medisterpølser* are fresh, unlinked pork sausages, usually flavoured with allspice, cloves, onion and black pepper. They are a Danish variation on Polish *kielbasa*, but without garlic.

The Low Countries – Belgium, Luxembourg and the Netherlands – have their sausage traditions as well. The forcemeat of Belgian *saucisse de choux* includes, as might be expected, cabbage; it

Assorted sausages, steaming hot, in Brussels.

is flavoured with marjoram, onion and sugar. Belgian black pudding, *bloed worst*, also contains a sweet spice: cinnamon. Like its French neighbours, Belgium enjoys its *boudin blanc* and *boudin noir*, but it also has its own variation, *boudin Liège*, a white sausage enhanced by generous amounts of fresh herbs (parsley and thyme) and *mirepoix*, a mixture of chopped celery, onion and carrots.

Bratwurst-like *Lëtzebuerger grillwurscht* ('Luxembourg grill sausages') were once known as *Thüringers* (a name now reserved for sausage that is made in Thuringia, in central Germany). *Träipen* are sweet sausages made of pork offal, trimmings and blood, bulked out with cabbage and breadcrumbs, and seasoned with caraway and honey. They are boiled, then fried, and served with apple sauce.

Dutch air-dried *metworst*, also known as *droge worst* ('dry sausage'), travelled to South Africa, where its name became *droëwors*, and the pork was replaced by types of game never seen in the Low Countries. It is unrelated to the similar-sounding German *Mettwurst*. Likewise, Dutch *braadworst* (roasted sausage) is different from German *Bratwurst*, although, to confuse matters, *Bratwurst* is sometimes called *braadworst* in Holland. Another name, *Duitse braadworst* – for the German variety – helps to clarify matters somewhat.

The Dutch favourite, *rookworst* (smoked sausage), is a smooth-textured sausage, like bologna or hot dogs, but formed in a horseshoe shape and seasoned very differently, more like a sausage from southern Italy, with garlic, fennel seeds, oregano, red pepper and wine vinegar. The traditional, or butcher's, version is encased in natural gut, while the mass-produced one comes in collagen casing and substitutes liquid smoke and preservatives for the time-consuming smoking process. The fresh ones should be simmered slowly, while the industrial ones need only a quick reheating.

Frikandellen are Dutch or Belgian skinless sausages, usually eaten with curried ketchup (like German *Currywurst*). Classic 'mystery meats', they may – and often do – contain some combination of chicken, beef, horse or pork. They are popular street food, in the home country as well as in Curaçao, in the Dutch West Indies. The South African *frikadel* (without an 'n') is not shaped like a sausage; it is a small patty or meatball of seasoned mince. Former Dutch colonies, such as Suriname, still consume their own versions of *vleesworst* (fresh white sausage, similar to *Weisswurst*) and *bloedworst*, blood sausage.

Balkenbrij is a scrapple-like sausage from Germany and the Netherlands. Offal – liver, lungs and kidneys – and seasonings (anise, cinnamon, cloves, ginger, liquorice, mace, sandalwood and sugar) are simmered in water to form a gelatine-rich stock. The stock and chopped meats are combined with wheat flour or oatmeal (in place of scrapple's cornmeal), then poured into loaf tins to cool and solidify. The type made in Gelderland is garnished with raisins. Once sliced and floured, *balkenbrij* is fried – just like scrapple.

Central Europe and the Balkans

Smoked Hungarian sausages include *csabai kolbász* or *csabai paprikás szalámi* (a spicy paprika-heavy variety, with caraway and cumin); *csemege kolbász* (with delicate sweet paprika); *cserkész kolbász* ('scout sausage', similar to 'foot-long' hot dogs, but dried); and *gyulai kolbász* (with both hot and sweet paprika, as well as sugar). In the less heavily smoked *debreceni kolbász*, marjoram is added to the usual garlic and paprika formula. *Rákóczi szalámi* is air-dried and laden with paprika; *téliszalámi* is a tangy air-cured salame; and *házi kolbász* is simply homemade sausage, always including paprika, but sometimes spiked with cloves or lemon zest.

The type of Polish sausage most often seen outside Poland is roughly patterned on *kielbasa starowiejska* (or *Polska kielbasa*) – smoked garlic sausage, formed into a loop or ring. In Poland, it is only one of several different types. *Krakowska kielbasa* is hot-smoked, and stuffed into a larger casing than other *kielbasas*. It includes allspice and coriander seeds as well as the usual garlic and pepper. Country-style *wiejska kielbasa* is made of veal seasoned with marjoram. No garlic flavours the air-dried, smoked *kabanosy* (usually just pepper, but sometimes caraway seeds). *Weselna kielbasa*, a dark, heavily smoked variety, is often served at weddings. Fresh, unsmoked *biala* ('white') *kielbasa* is still garlicky, but derives its aromatic herbal quality from marjoram.

A hunter's version of *ćevapčići* from Albania, Bosnia-Herzegovina, Croatia, Macedonia or Serbia might contain rabbit or venison. Traditionally grilled on skewers, *ćevapčići* are redolent of garlic and onion, although local variations include allspice, celery leaves, chillies, parsley, red wine, rosemary or thyme.

Kulen are salami-like sausages from Croatia and Serbia. They come in two sizes, stuffed into either hog casings or hog middles. Spiced with garlic and hot paprika, they are sold fresh, smoked or cured. The last may be covered with white mould, and some are even buried in ashes to speed up the drying process.

Russia and the Former USSR

Cooked sausages include doctor's sausage (similar to *mortadella*); Moscow sausage (wild boar, finely ground, flavoured with cloves, orange rind and *kümmel*, caraway-infused vodka); *teewurst* (much like the spreadable German sausage); and, of course, hot dogs.

Semi-smoked sausages include *poltava* (a garlicky Ukrainian ring sausage, similar to *kielbasa*); *Semipalatinsk* (containing as much as 20 per cent offal, and named after a giant former nuclear testing site); as well as other Russian regional types, from Arzamas, and from former members of the USSR: Belarus (Minsk), Georgia (Tbilisi), Lithuania, Poland (Krakow) and Ukraine (Donbas, Drohobych, Kiev).

Hunter's sausage, a dry sausage made of pork and beef, seasoned with juniper; Moscow sausage, which is both cooked and smoked; Soviet sausage, not just a metaphorical sausage, but like *kielbasa* save for its distinctly red pellicle; and tourist sausages, small smoked links flavoured with caraway and garlic, are all smoked.

Special sausages, in Russia, are similar to other Eastern European types: blood sausages (virtually identical to Polish *kiszka*), brawn and spreadable liver sausages, like *Braunschweiger*.

The United States and the New World

Cajun *boudin rouge* is descended from the French *boudin noir*; it is still blood sausage, but spicier than its ancestor. Eliminating the blood and adding pig's heart and liver produces Cajun *boudin blanc*. If *boudin blanc* forcemeat is rolled into a meatball, dipped in batter and deep-fried, it makes a *boudin* ball. *Boudin* does not *have* to be made of pork; popular *boudins* use indigenous meats from the bayous: crayfish and alligator. *Andouille* and *chaurice* are also Cajun classics. The French *andouille* evolved into a different species of sausage in the bayous: spicier and all pork, it leaves out the tripe used in the original. *Chaurice* is similar to Spanish chorizo, but is hotter and has hints of thyme and allspice not found in Spain.

Besides hot dogs, 'Italian sausage' (like *luganega*, but with added red pepper and fennel seeds) and pepperoni, the most common sausage is simply called 'breakfast sausage' or 'country sausage'. Available in links (either hog casings or smaller sheep casings), or as a small log covered with plastic, they are frequently served as fried patties. Their primary seasonings are salt, pepper and sage, and sometimes marjoram and allspice. The English sage-flavoured sausage tradition (such as Cumberland sausage) is in the genes of American breakfast patties.

All over Latin America, variations on the *morcilla* theme are popular: Uruguayans make something similar to the San Franciscan *biroldo*, but flavoured with chocolate and garnished with dried fruit, orange zest or peanuts; Chileans call theirs *prieta*; and Ecuadorians, *salchicha*. Other local Spanish names include *rellena*, 'stuffed', and *tubería negra*, 'black tubing'.

Brazilian *linguiça* is made of pork flesh, while their *chouriço* uses the blood of pigs. In the Caribbean, Dominicans and Puerto Ricans make a different distinction: *longaniza* is a dried, cured sausage, while chorizo is smoked. In Ecuador local *longaniza* is smoked, but chorizo is imported from Spain. Contrary to expectation, the most popular Ecuadorian sausage is neither chorizo nor *longaniza* – it is (you guessed it) the hot dog.

Argentina's *chorizo criollo* is not like the dried chorizo of Spain, nor the crumbly and highly spiced chorizo of Mexico. It is unfermented and seasoned with garlic, nutmeg, red wine, sugar and pepper (both ground and, as garnish, whole). It is a fresh sausage, usually sliced and fried. Sweet anise seeds perfume Argentinian *longanizas*. Their *morcilla* adds liver and tongue to the familiar blood sausage, as well as garlic, onions and oregano – quite different from Spanish *morcilla*.

References

1 What is Sausage, and Where Did it Originate?

1 Jean Bottéro, *The Oldest Cuisine in the World: Cooking in Mesopotamia* (Chicago and London, 2004), pp. 59–60.
2 Maguelonne Toussaint-Samat, *A History of Food*, trans. Anthea Bell (Cambridge, MA, 1992), p. 440.
3 Drew Magary, 'Tuesday Watch List: Romney Gets Silly!', NBC, 30 May 2012, online at www.nbcphiladelphia.com.
4 Paul S. Cohen, 'The Genuine Etymological Story of Phon(c)y', *Transactions of the Philological Society*, CIX/1, p. 6.
5 Dr Jean Bordeaux, quoted in Eric Partridge, *A Dictionary of Slang and Unconventional English* (New York, 1961), p. 76.
6 'Sausage Reigns Supreme in New Poll', 3 October 2011, online at www.marketwatch.com.
7 Quoted in Doug Gelbert, 'Baseball and Hotdogs: The Origins of Both American Institutions Are Shrouded in Mystery', 6 March 2006, online at www.ezinearticles.com.
8 Bret Thorn, 'Chefs Go Whole Hog for Charcuterie', *Nation's Restaurant News*, 16 November 2011, online at www.nrn.com.

3 Sausages of Europe

1 Ivan Day, 'Some Interesting English Puddings', *Historic Food*, online at www.historicfood.com, accessed December 2014.

4 Sausages from Everywhere Else

1 Peter G. Rose, *The Sensible Cook: Dutch Foodways in the Old and the New World* (Syracuse, NY, 1989), pp. 93–4.

5 Technology and the Modern Sausage

1 Anne Mendelson, personal correspondence.
2 Roger Tuma, 'The Poison that Heals', 26 February 2011, online at www.english.pravda.ru.
3 Richard A. Scanlan, 'Nitrosamines and Cancer', Linus Pauling Institute, November 2000, online at http://lpi.oregonstate.edu.
4 L. Wendell Haymon, 'Bacterial Fermentations, Sodium Acid Pyrophosphate and Glucono Delta Lactone in Cured Sausage Production', American Meat Science Association, *Reciprocal Meat Conference Proceedings*, XXXIV (1981), online at www.eurekamag.com.

6 Sausage: Theme and Variations

1 Calvin W. Schwabe, *Unmentionable Cuisine* (Charlottesville, VA, 1979), p. 118.
2 Peter Lund Simmons, *The Curiosities of Food: Or the Dainties and Delicacies of the Different Nations Obtained from the Animal Kingdom* [1859] (Berkeley, CA, 2001), p. 104.
3 Frederick J. Simoons, *Eat Not This Flesh: Food Avoidances from Prehistory to the Present* (Madison, WI, 1994), p. 106. Polonies

are English sausages, more typically made of partly
cooked beef (and sometimes pork), that look like short,
fat frankfurters. The name is a corruption of 'bologna'.

4 Ibid., p. 190.

5 Schwabe, *Unmentionable Cuisine*, p. 104.

6 Quoted in Simmons, *Curiosities of Food*, p. 80.

7 Platina (Bartolomeo Sacchi), *De honesta voluptate et valetudinae*
[1465], quoted in Harold McGee, *On Food and Cooking: The
Science and Lore of the Kitchen*, 2nd ed. (New York, 2004),
p. 169.

8 Ludovicus Nonnius, *Diaeticon*, quoted in Sarah T. Peterson,
Acquired Taste: The French Origins of Modern Cooking (Ithaca,
NY, 1994), p. 90.

Conclusion

1 H. L. Mencken, *A Second Mencken Chrestomathy* (Baltimore,
MD, 2006), p. 423.

Select Bibliography

Aristophanes, *The Knights*, online at http://classics.mit.edu

Athenaeus, *The Deipnosophists*, online at http://penelope.
uchicago.edu

Barlow, John, *Everything but the Squeal: Eating the Whole Hog
in Northern Spain* (New York, 2008)

Bottéro, Jean, *The Oldest Cuisine in the World: Cooking in
Mesopotamia* (Chicago and London, 2004)

Child, Lydia Maria, *The American Frugal Housewife* (Mineola,
NY, 1999)

Davidson, Alan, ed., *The Oxford Companion to Food*
(Oxford, 1999)

Day, Ivan, 'Some Interesting English Puddings', *Historic Food*,
online at www.historicfood.com (accessed December 2014)

Figge, Katrin, 'Currywurst: Far More Than Just a Sausage',
Jakarta Globe, 1 November 2011, online at www.
thejakartaglobeberitasatu.com

Freedman, Paul, ed., *Food: The History of Taste* (Berkeley,
CA, 2007)

Glasse, Hannah, *The Art of Cookery Made Plain and Easy* (1747),
online at www.celtnet.org.uk (accessed December 2014)

Grigson, Jane, *The Art of Charcuterie* (New York, 1968)

——, *Charcuterie and French Pork Cookery* (London, 2001)

Grocock, Christopher, and Sally Grainger, *Apicius: A Critical
Edition with an Introduction and English Translation* (Totnes,
Devon, 2006)

Henderson, Fergus, *Nose to Tail Eating: A Kind of British Cooking* (New York, 2004)

Karmas, Endel, *Sausage Processing* (Park Ridge, NJ, 1972)

Kraig, Bruce, *Hot Dog: A Global History* (London, 2009)

——, and Patty Carroll, *Man Bites Dog: Hot Dog Culture in America* (Lanham, MD, 2014)

Kutas, Rytek, *Great Sausage Recipes and Meat Curing* (Buffalo, NY, 1984)

Lissner, Erich, *Wurstologia, oder Es Geht um die Wurst* (Wiesbaden-Biebrich, 1939)

McGee, Harold, *On Food and Cooking: The Science and Lore of the Kitchen*, 2nd ed. (New York, 2004)

Mencken, H. L., *A Second Mencken Chrestomathy* (Baltimore, MD, 2006)

Merinoff, Linda, *The Savory Sausage: A Culinary Tour Around the World* (New York, 1987)

Mueller, T. G., *The Professional Chef's Book of Charcuterie* (New York, 1987)

Nollet, Leo M. L., and Fidel Toldrá, *Advanced Technologies for Meat Processing* (Boca Raton, FL, 2006)

Ockerman, Herbert W., and Lopa Basu, 'Fermented Meat Products: Production and Consumption' (Columbus, OH, n.d.), online at https://kb.osu.edu

Partridge, Eric, *A Dictionary of Slang and Unconventional English* (New York, 1961)

Peterson, Sarah T., *Acquired Taste: The French Origins of Modern Cooking* (Ithaca, NY, 1994)

Petronius Arbiter, *The Satyricon* [fourth/fifth century CE], trans. W. C. Firebaugh, online at www.gutenberg.org

Philogelos (fourth/fifth century AD), online at http://publishing.yudu.com

Platina (Bartolomeo Sacchi), *De honesta voluptate et valetudinae* [1465], in Harold McGee, *On Food and Cooking: The Science and Lore of the Kitchen*, 2nd edn (New York, 2004)

Randolph, Mary, *The Virginia Housewife; or, Methodical Cook* (1824) (New York, 1993)

Rose, Peter G., *The Sensible Cook: Dutch Foodways in the Old and the*

New World (Syracuse, NY, 1989)

Schwabe, Calvin W., *Unmentionable Cuisine* (Charlottesville, VA, 1979)

Simmons, Peter Lund, *The Curiosities of Food: Or the Dainties and Delicacies of the Different Nations Obtained from the Animal Kingdom* [1859] (Berkeley, CA, 2001)

Simoons, Frederick J., *Eat Not This Flesh: Food Avoidances from Prehistory to the Present* (Madison, WI, 1994)

Toussaint-Samat, Maguelonne, *A History of Food*, trans. Anthea Bell (Cambridge, MA, 1992)

Waddington, Keir, 'The Dangerous Sausage Diet: Meat and Disease in Victorian and Edwardian Britain', *Cultural and Social History*, VIII/1 (2011), pp. 51–71

Wise, Victoria, *American Charcuterie: Recipes from Pig-by-the-Tail* (New York, 1986)

Wright, Clifford A., 'Sausage Peddlers, Vagabonds, and Bandits', online at www.cliffordawright.com (accessed December 2014)

Zaouali, Lilia, *Medieval Cuisine of the Islamic World* (Berkeley, CA, 2007)

Websites and Associations

Clay's Kitchen: Sausage Recipes
www.panix.com/~clay

Homemade-Sausage.net
www.homemade-sausage.net

Salumi Casalinghi Forum
www.sossai.net

Sausage Debauchery
www.sausagedebauchery.blogspot.co.uk

Sausage Fans
www.sausagefans.co.uk

Sausage Making
www.sausagemaking.org

SausageMania
www.sausagemania.com

Sonoma Mountain Sausages
http://lpoli.50webs.com

Acknowledgements

This book is the product of the expertise and support of many people, and would not exist without their contributions. They deserve all the credit for its strengths. The blame for its weaknesses I reserve for myself.

I have first to thank Ken Albala, historian of all things culinary, who practises what he preaches. He put me in touch with Jeremy Fletcher, who has collected and translated a vast number of medieval and Renaissance sausage recipes. I learned an incredible amount from former colleagues at the Culinary Institute of America, whose collective culinary experience and generosity of spirit always exceeded even my greediest expectations – especially Bob del Grosso, who has gone on to become a master of artisanal charcuterie.

The book would not look nearly as nice had it not been for images graciously provided by Cynthia Bertelsen, Warren Bobrow, Alessandro Morreale, Grace Piper, Karen Resta and Scott Stegen. It would have been impossible without the assistance of libraries, and I spent many productive hours in the Conrad N. Hilton Library of the Culinary Institute of America, the Sojourner Truth Library of the State University of New York College at New Paltz, and the New York Public Library.

I am indebted for their generous contributions to Judith Jones, Anne Mendelson, Bruce Kraig, Andrew Smith and numerous members of the Association for the Study of Food and Society, who never failed to provide answers when I couldn't find them myself.

Rick Kelly first drew my attention to Native American blood sausage. Deborah Begley and Tamara Watson not only plied me with great food and wine, but also served them up with wit and intelligence. Aaron Rester and Kate Krajci – despite their vegetarian proclivities – aided and abetted my activities in Chicago (a place that Sandburg might well have called the 'City of the Big Sausages').

So many others should be listed here that, had they been included, a second volume would have been required. Nonetheless, I would be a fool if I did not acknowledge the contributions of my wife, Karen, whose support and wry humour, tempered by wholly justified scepticism (and a seemingly incompatible willingness to try whatever weird things appeared on our table), made this book possible. I solemnly promise that she will not have to eat sausages every day *this* year.

Photo Acknowledgements

The author and the publishers wish to express their thanks to the below sources of illustrative material and/or permission to reproduce it.

Gary Allen: pp. 13, 90, 98, 101 bottom, 117; William Avery: p. 31; Cynthia Bertelsen: pp. 11, 27, 30, 48, 49, 103, 108; © The Trustees of the British Museum, London: p. 56; Jdvillalobos: pp. 46, 71; Steve Evans: p. 78; hongnhung106: p. 79; iStockphoto: p. 6 (Lauri-Patterson); kallerna: p. 136; Library of Congress, Washington, DC: p. 83; Alessandro Morreale: pp. 14, 45 bottom, 105, 109, 110, 129; André Mouraux: p. 137; National Gallery of Art, Washington, DC: p. 85; Véronique Pagnier: p. 134; Alefirenko Petro: p. 99; Grace Piper: p. 84 top; Collection of Karen Resta: pp. 18, 22, 66; Mo Riza: p. 76; Salimfadhley: p. 8; Seydelmann: p. 86 top; Scott Stegen: pp. 45 top, 101 top; Shutterstock: p. 113 (Dulce Rubia); Southern Arkansas University: p. 65; Takeaway: p. 77; Thelmadatter: p. 70; U.S. Patent 3,152,359, 13 October 1964: p. 89; U.S. Patent 3,583,023, 8 June 1971: p. 91; Vinhtantran: p. 111.

Index

italic numbers refer to illustrations; **bold** to recipes